30 Days of Coloring Books for Kids and Adults

Book 4

Patterns

By Gary Wittmann

First Published, 2018

Printed in the United States of America

Please use light color pencil or crayons or fine markers, there is a blank page following the drawing. You may wish to put something under the page to prevent bleeding.

Thanks for buying this ebook.

Join us on Facebook:

https://www.facebook.com/30DaysofColoringBooksForKidsandAdults/

We will start to have some Facebook Live Coloring Pages.

This link will help your sign up to our newsletter.

http://bit.ly/2C92vYS

copy and paste into your browser.

Reasons to play with Coloring books.

1. **Coloring helps you unwind.**

   Let's face it—at the end of the day our lives are filled with deadlines. Sitting down and just unwind with our creative process helps us.

2. **Coloring stimulates your right brain and helps you think more clearly.**

   Research shows you are more creative when your right brain is stimulated.

3. **Coloring makes for a fun night in with friends.**

   Great time is with your family or friends doing what you may in loving to draw and talk and have fun.

4. **Coloring is a great creative outlet.**

   It doesn't matter about your artistic ability. It doesn't matter about your letting the sky be blue or green. You get to do what you feel.

5. **Coloring books makes the perfect gift.**

   Recently at a get together, I had a present for everyone who came to our party. It was a box of coloring books and crayons and markers. Everyone laugh so hard and talk more than if we were playing cards.

Join us on Facebook:

https://www.facebook.com/30DaysofColoringBooksForKidsandAdults/

We will start to have some Facebook Live

Coloring Pages.

We will also be starting an Etsy Store for individual

pages.

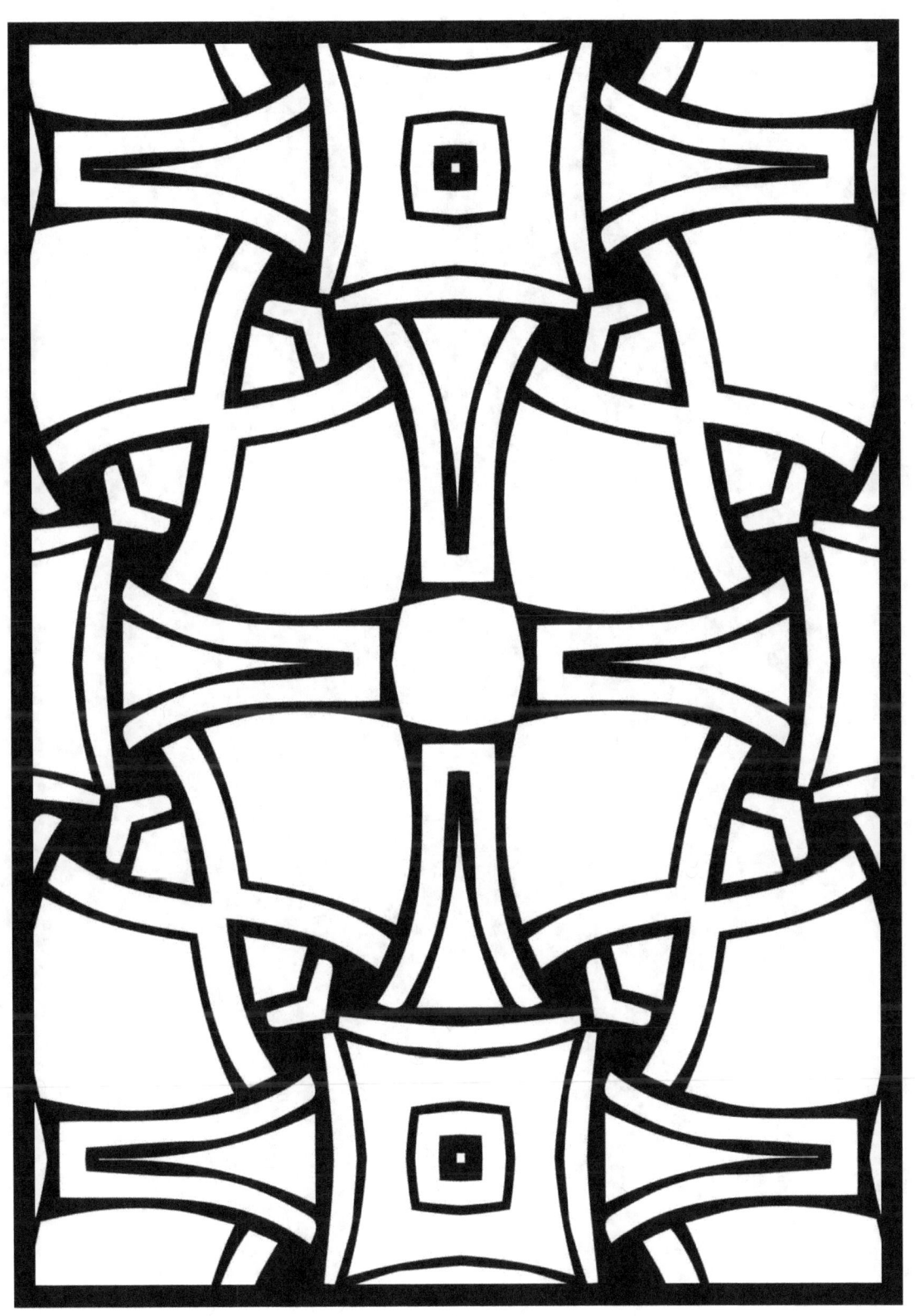

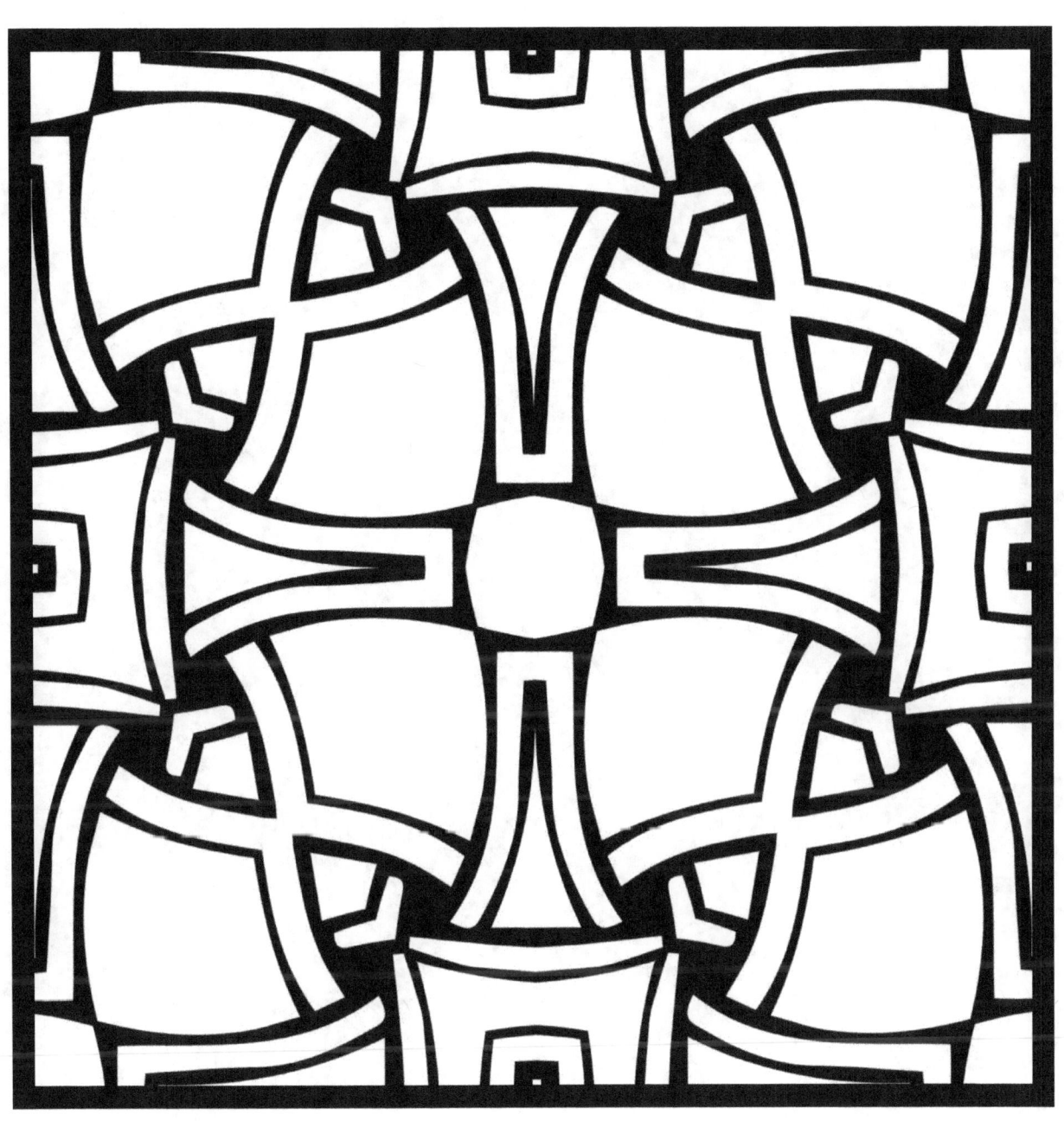

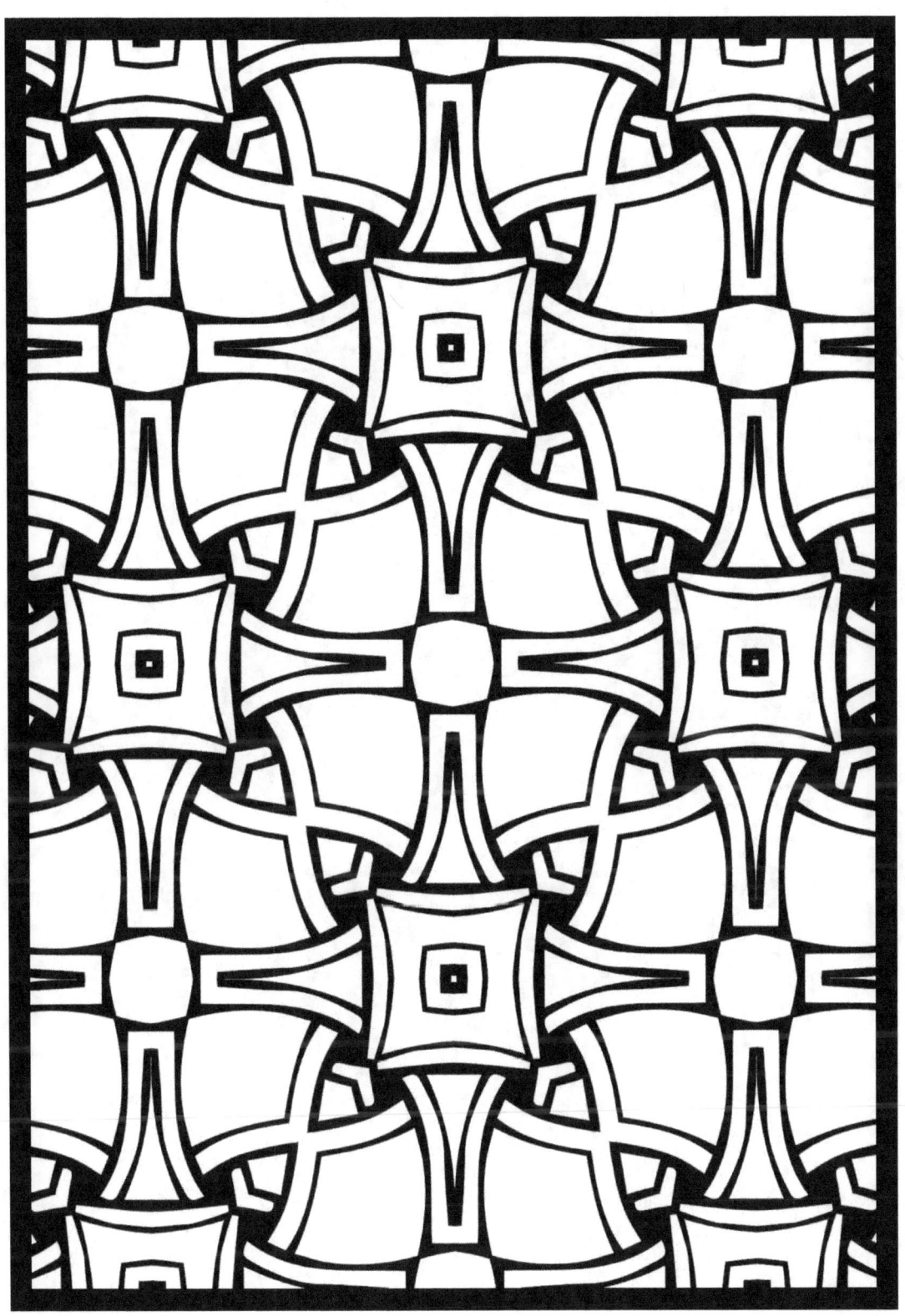

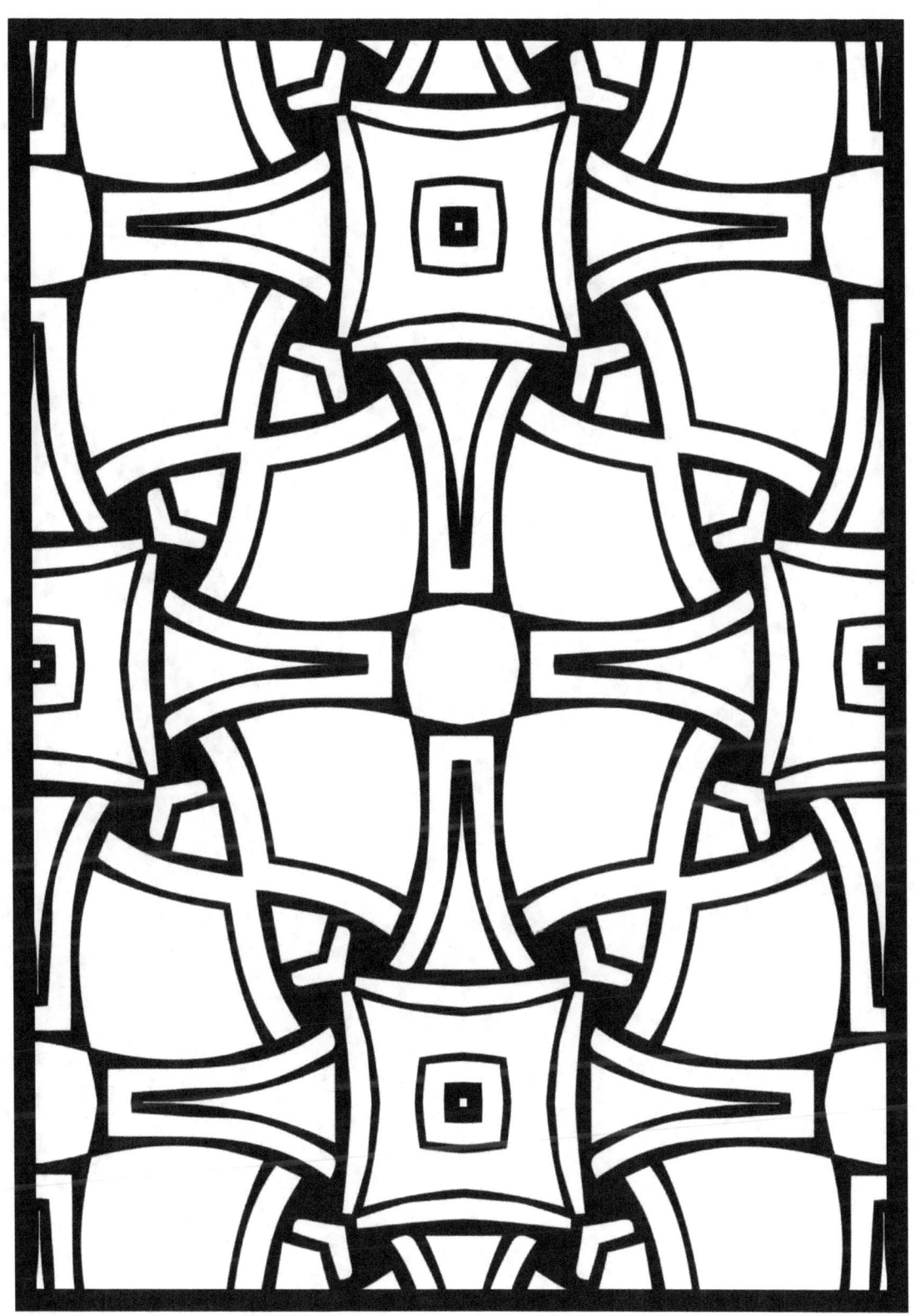

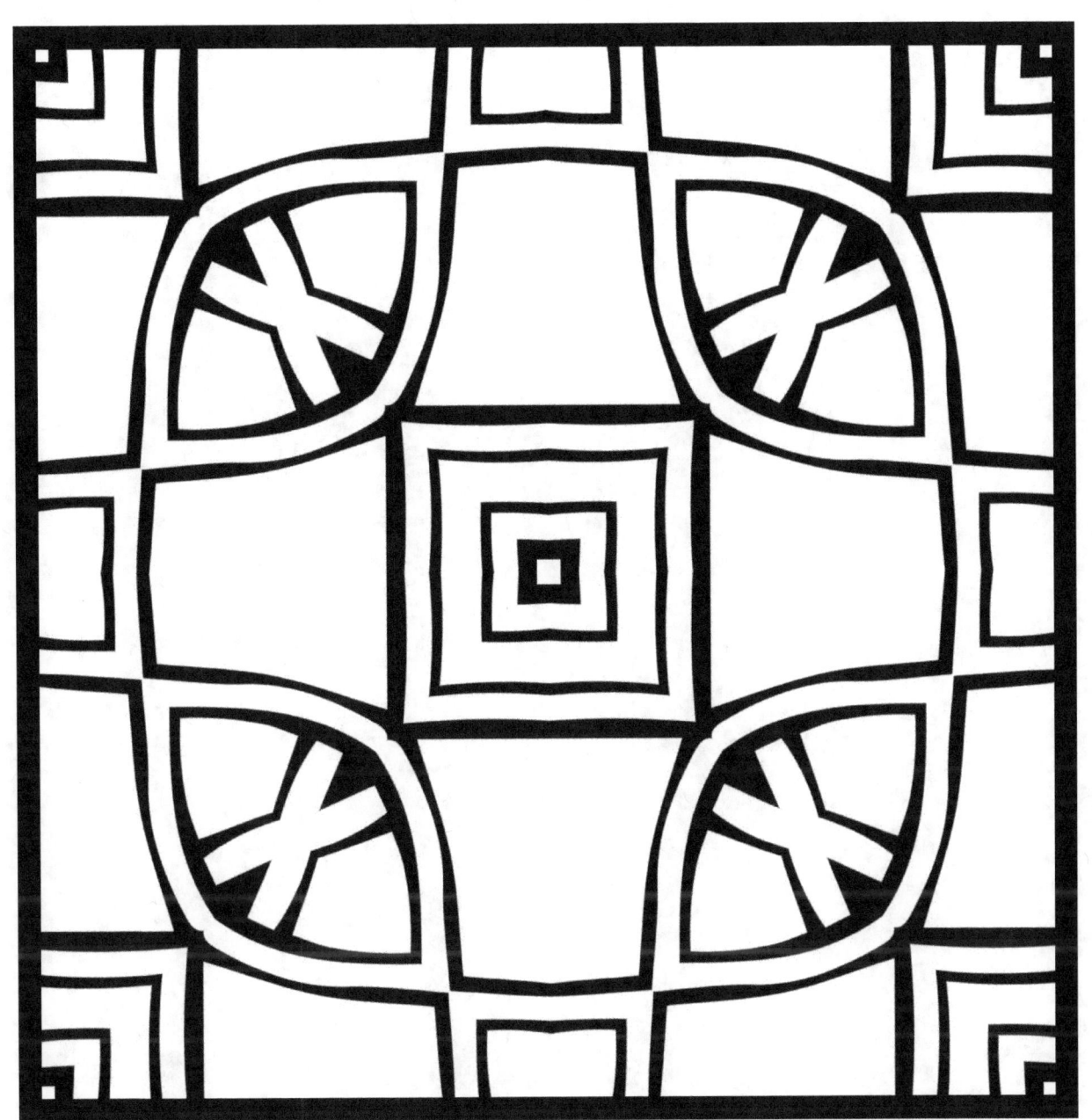

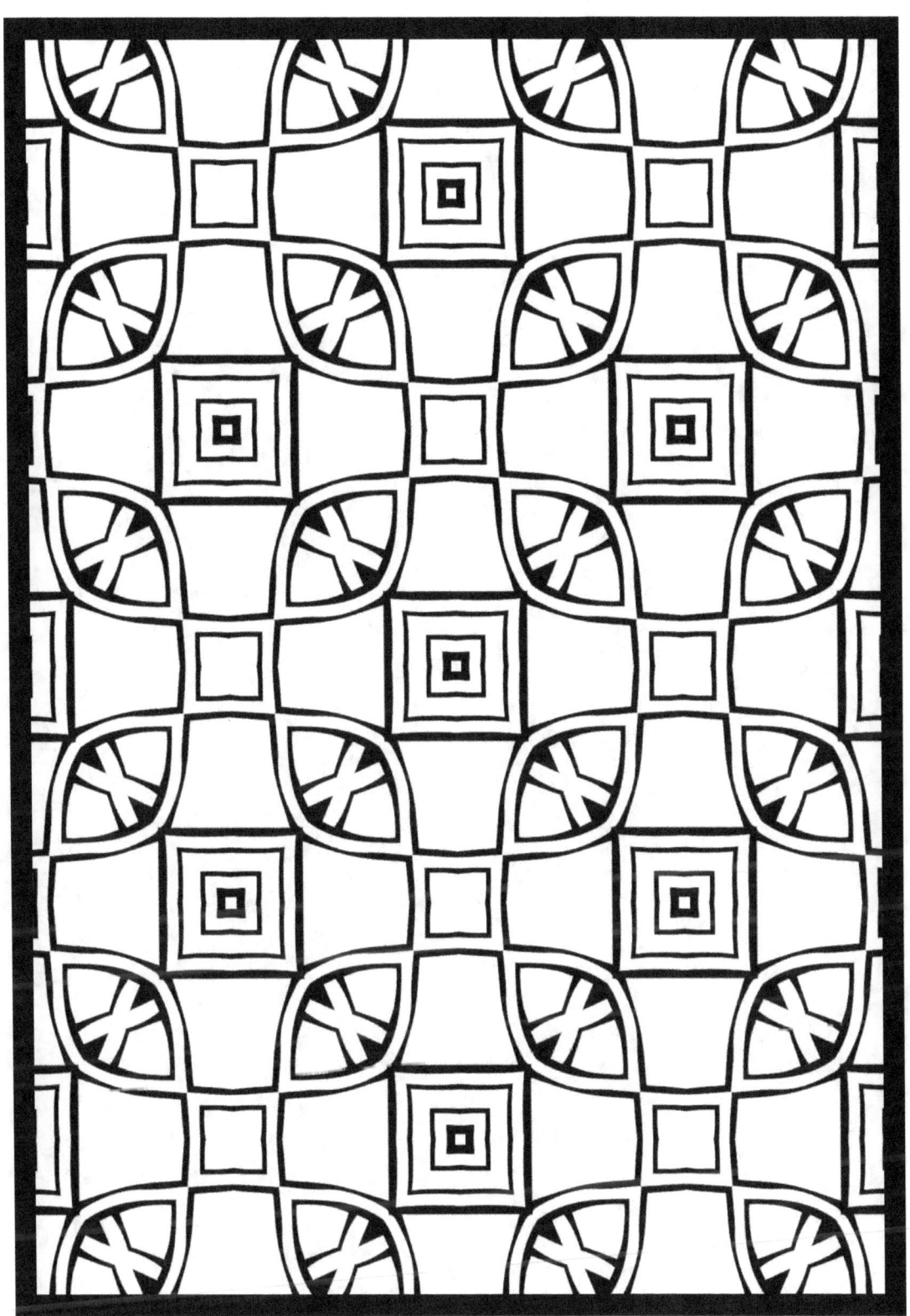

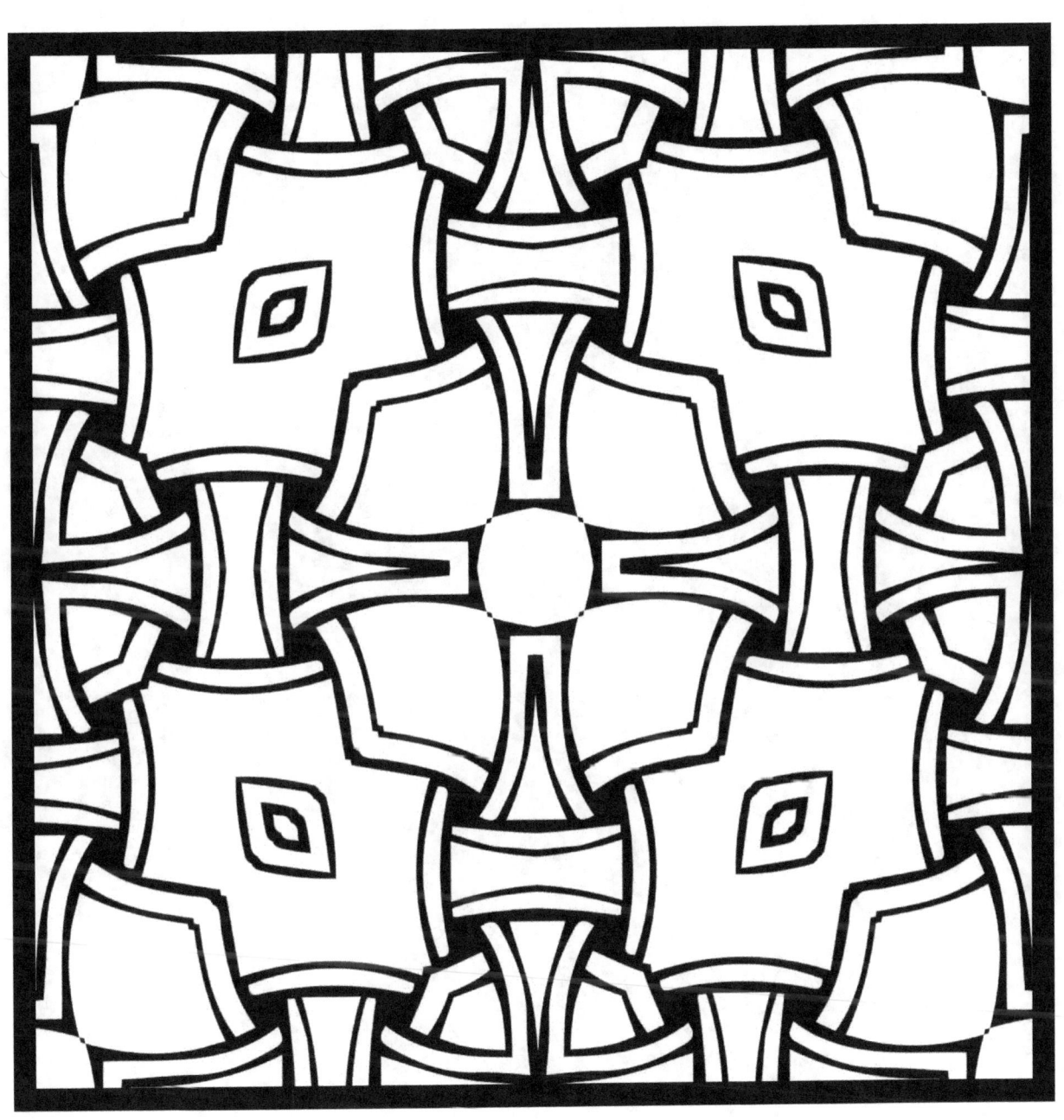

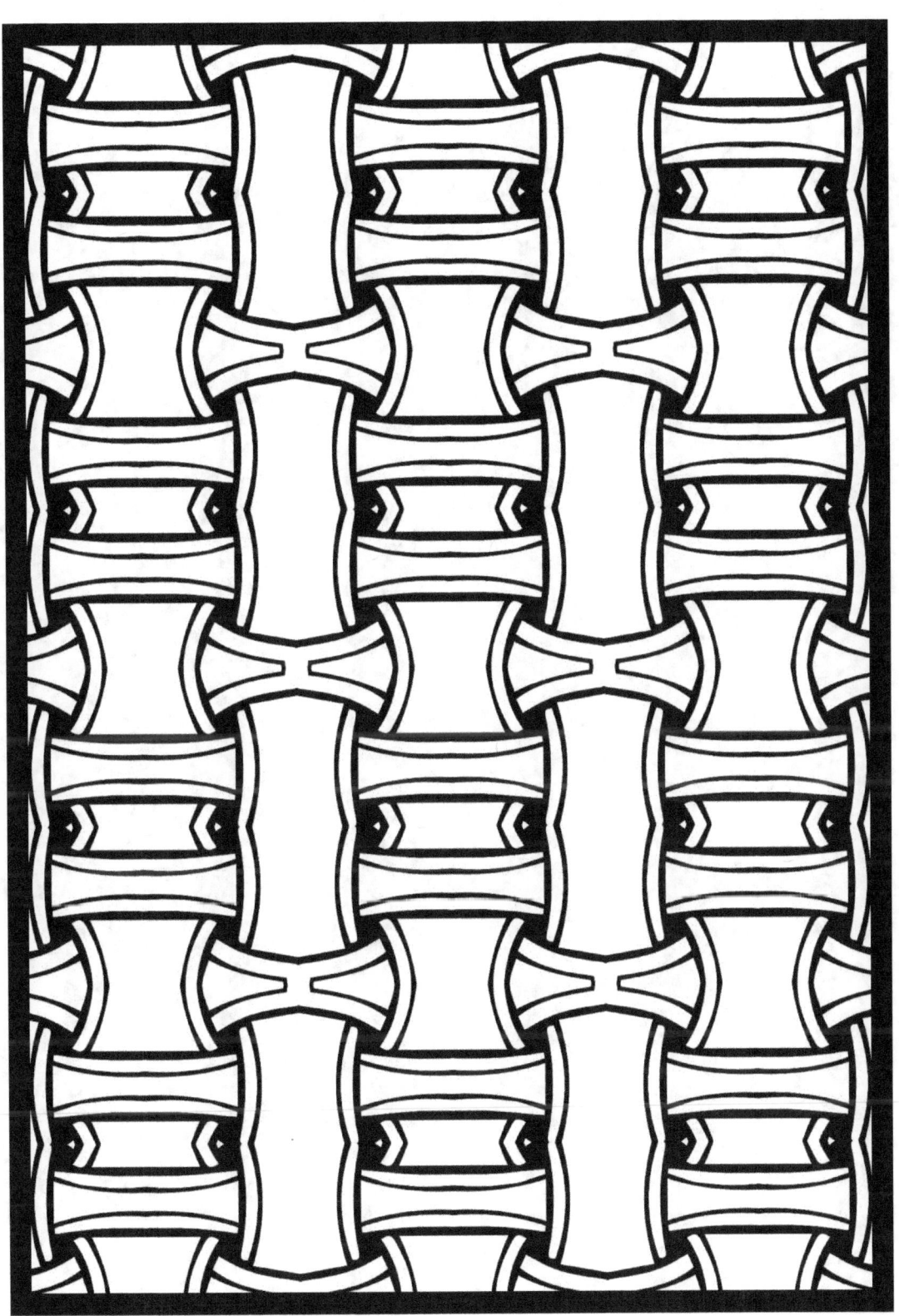

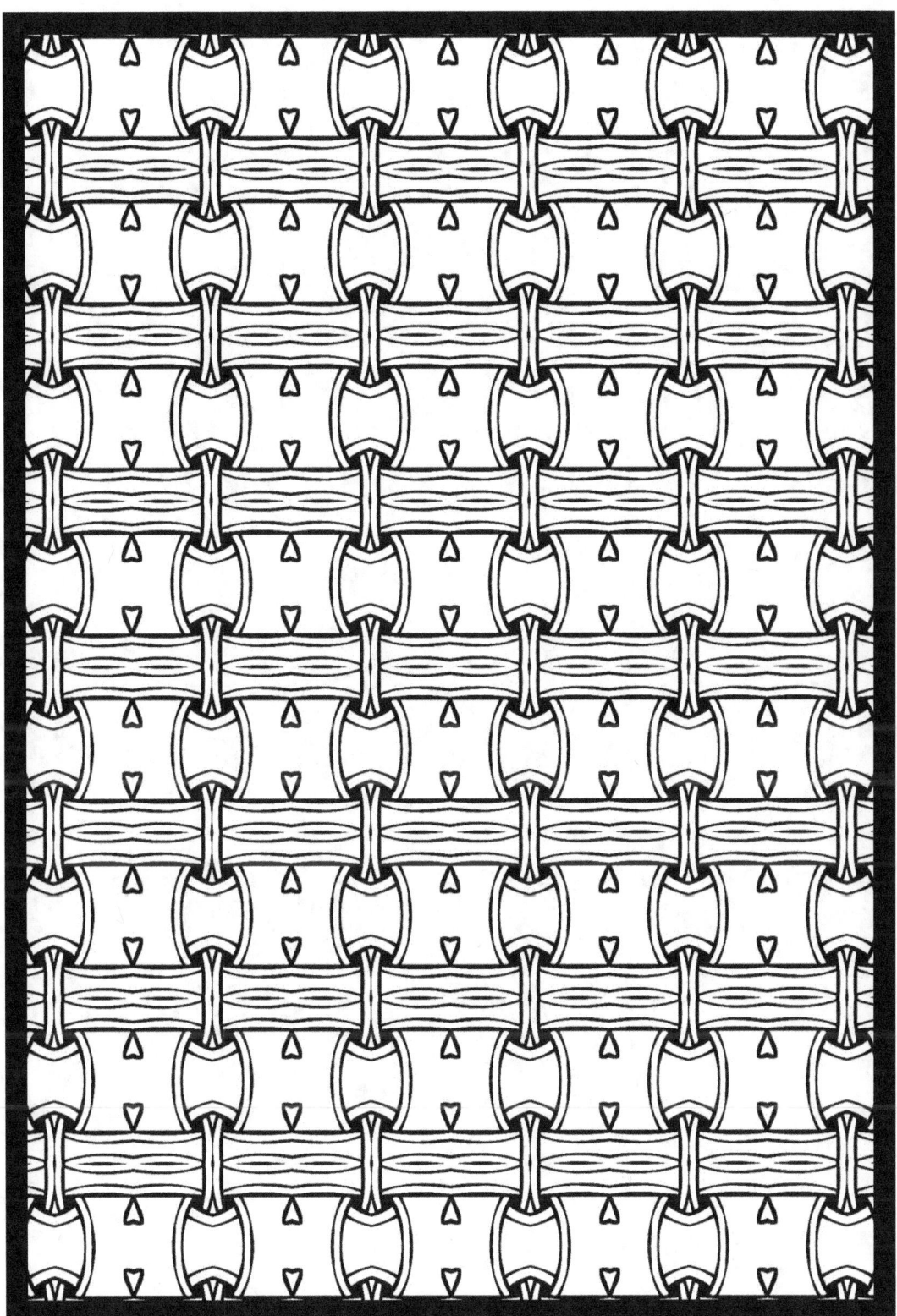

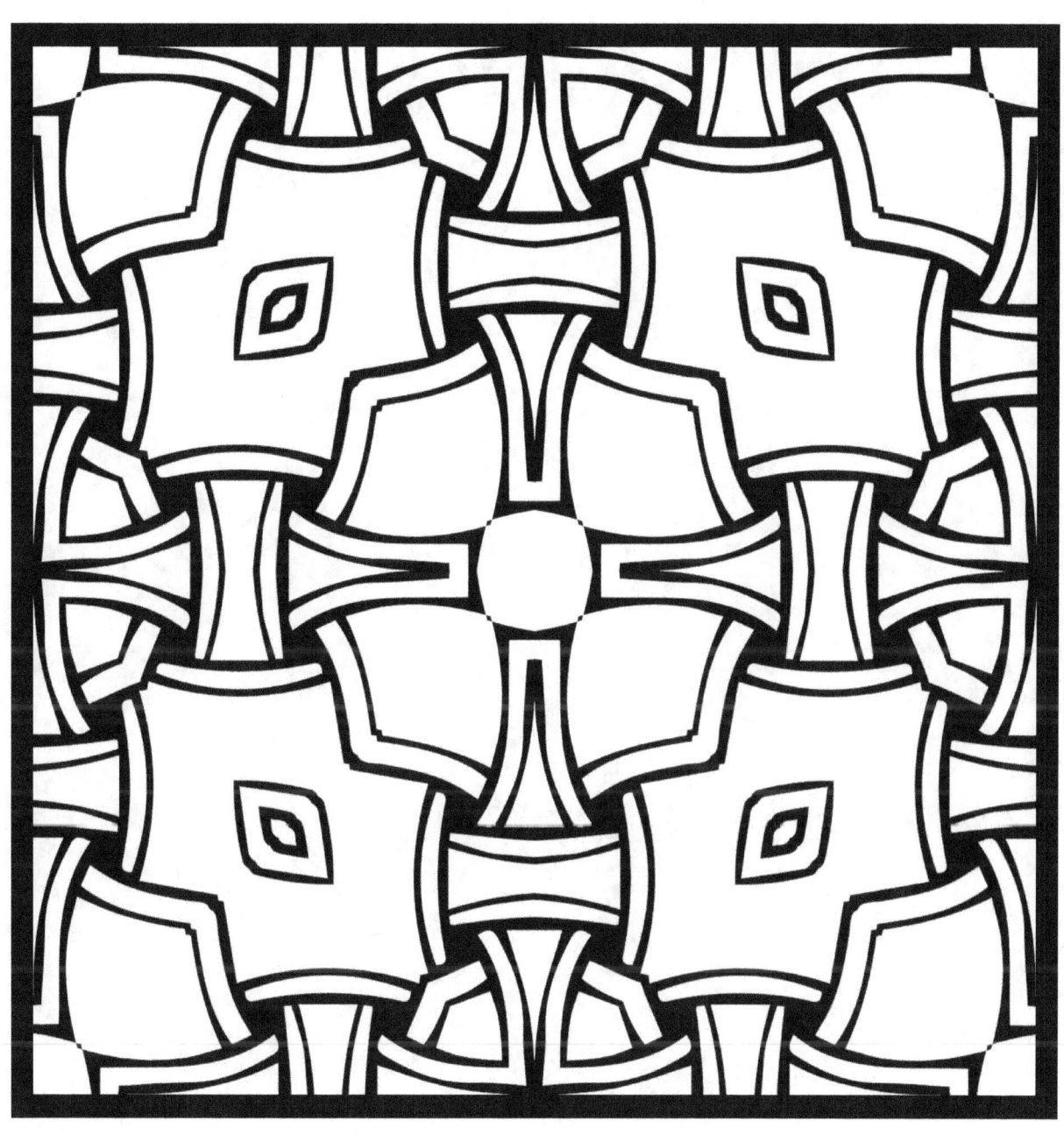

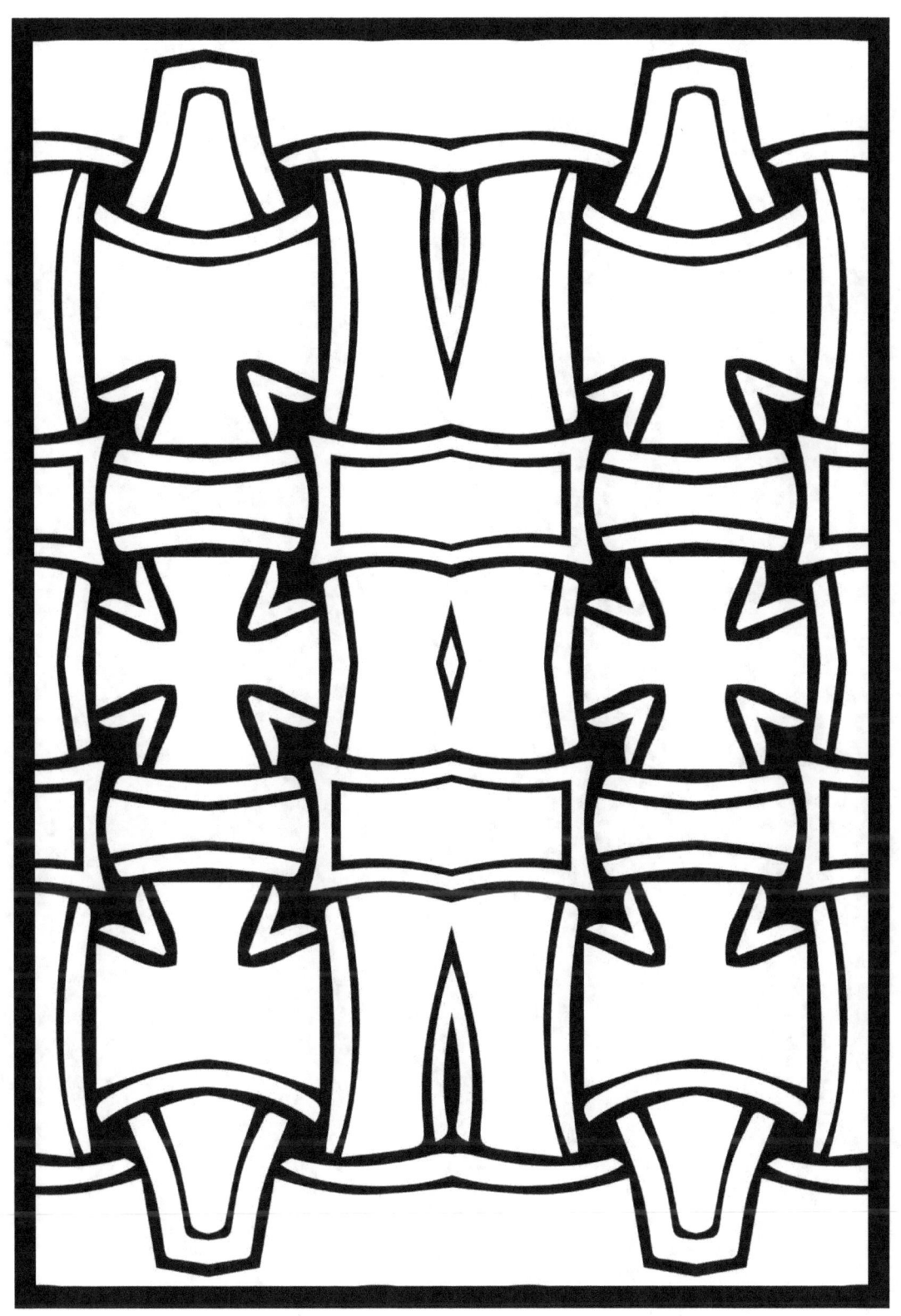

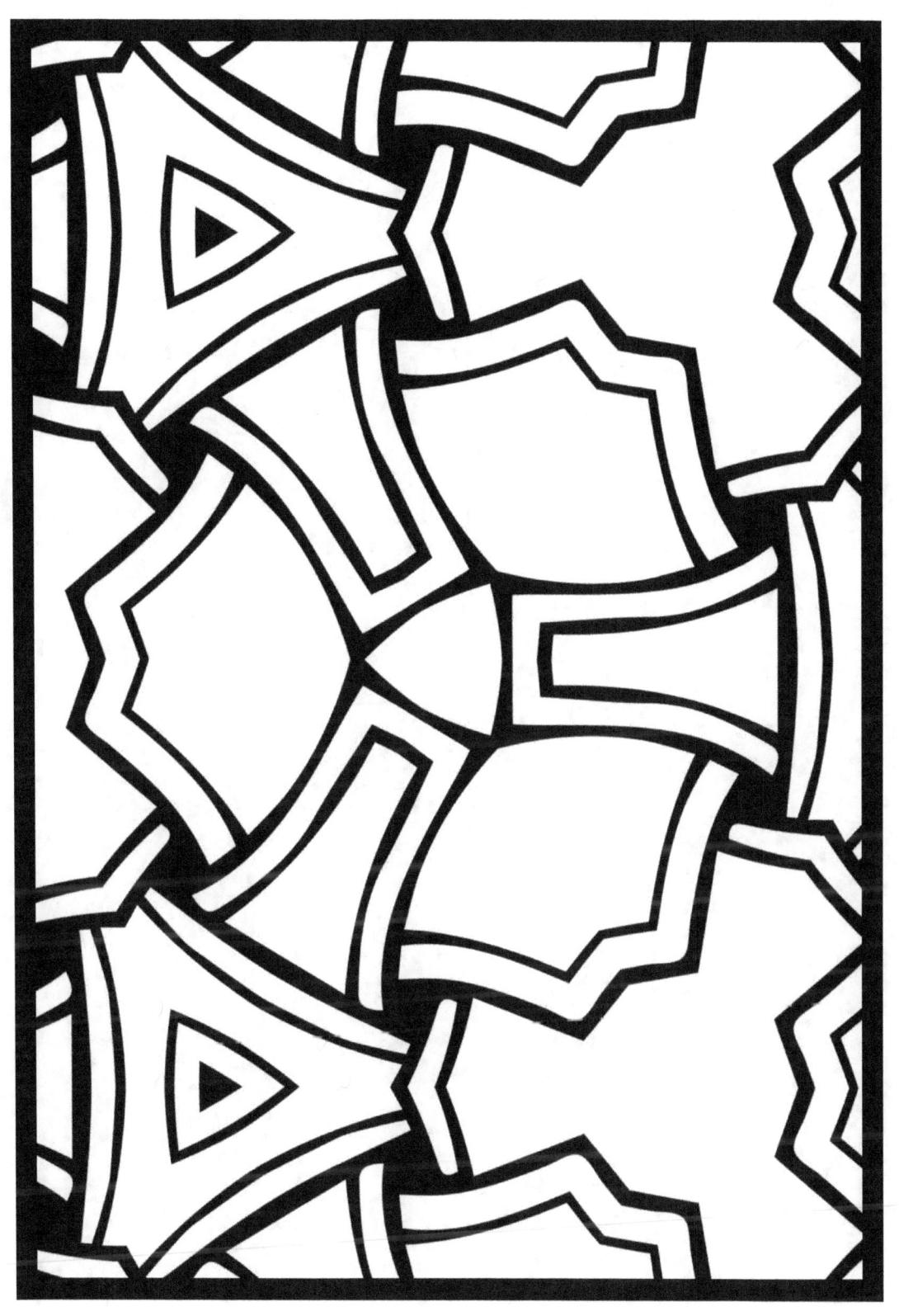

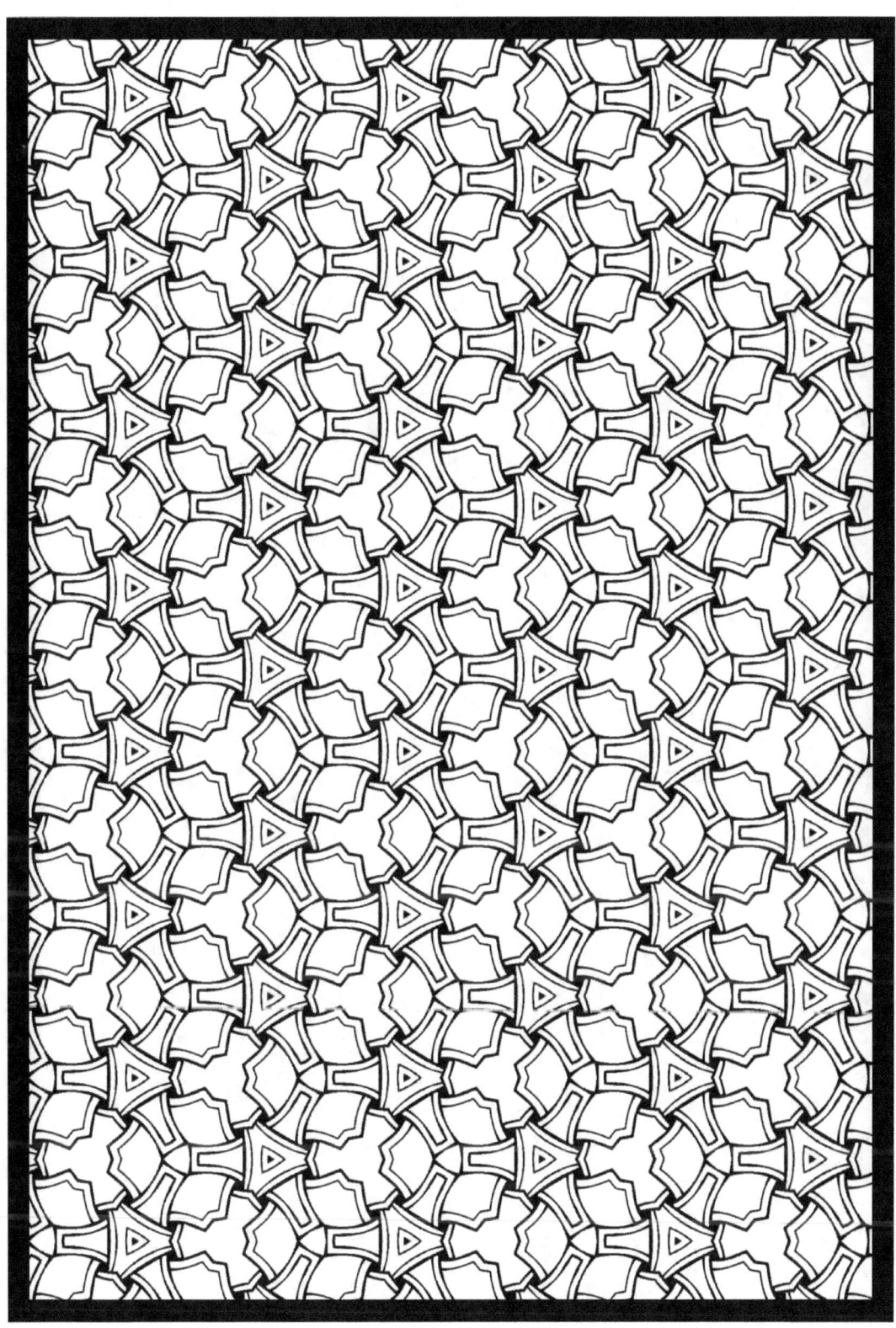

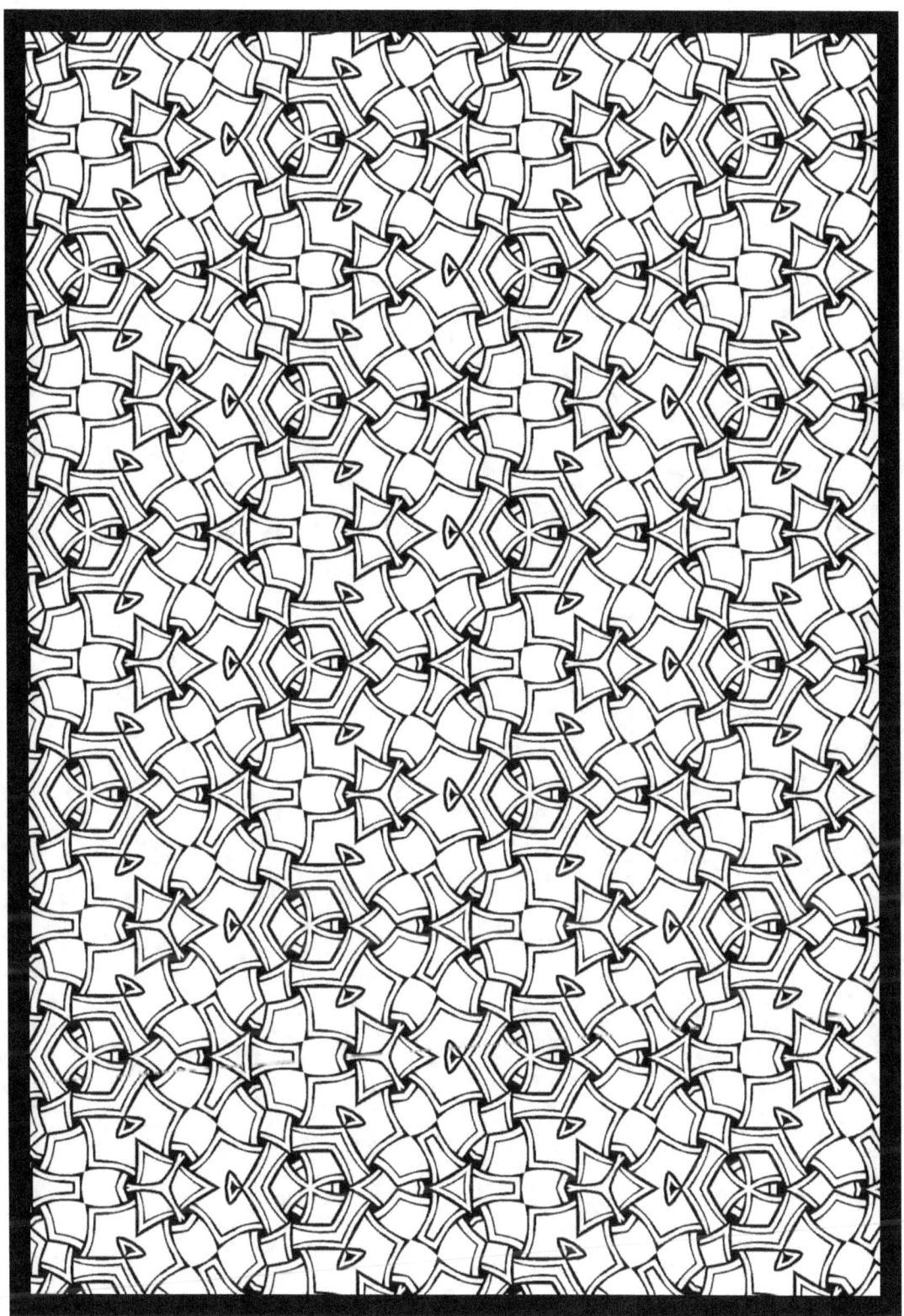

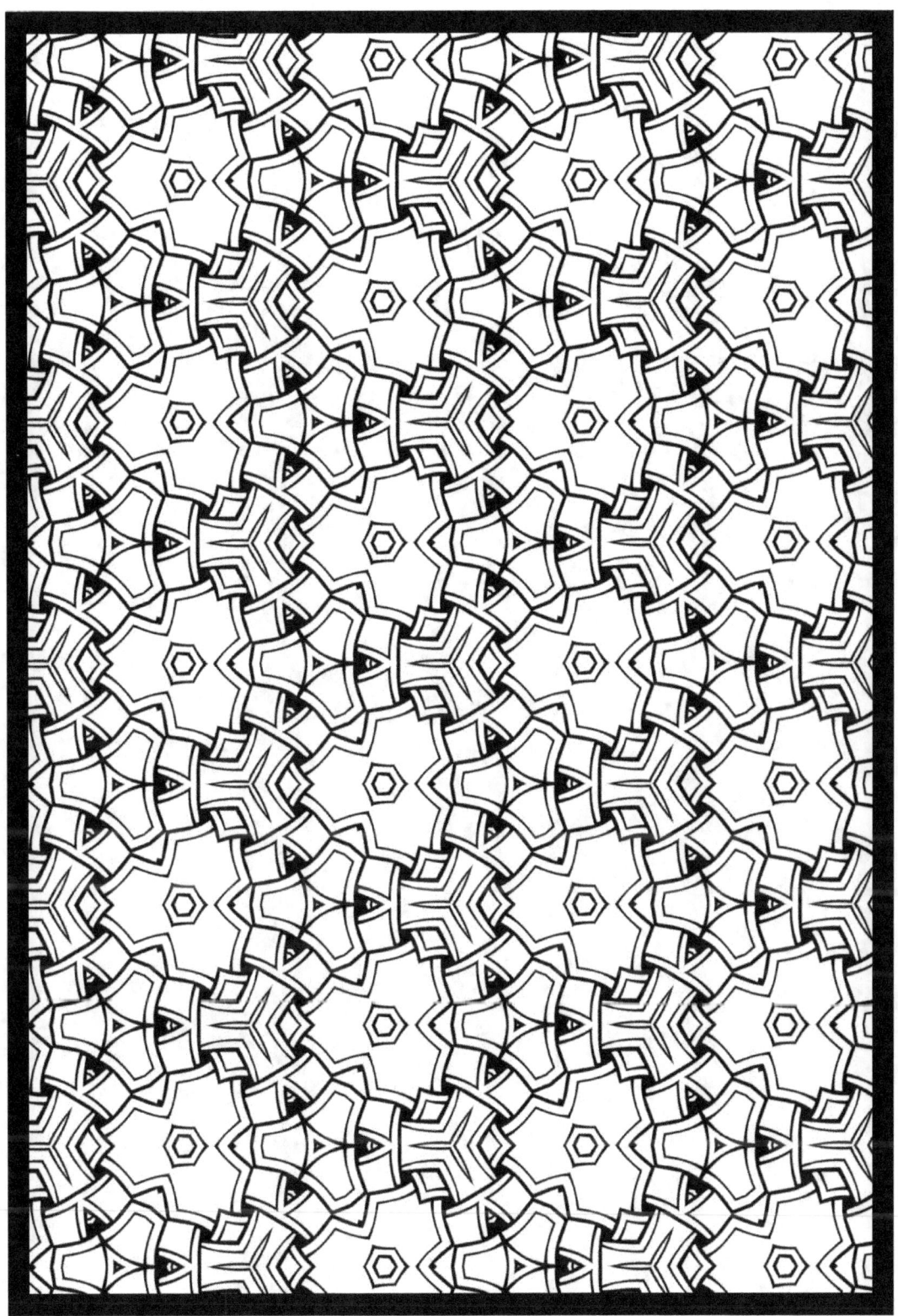

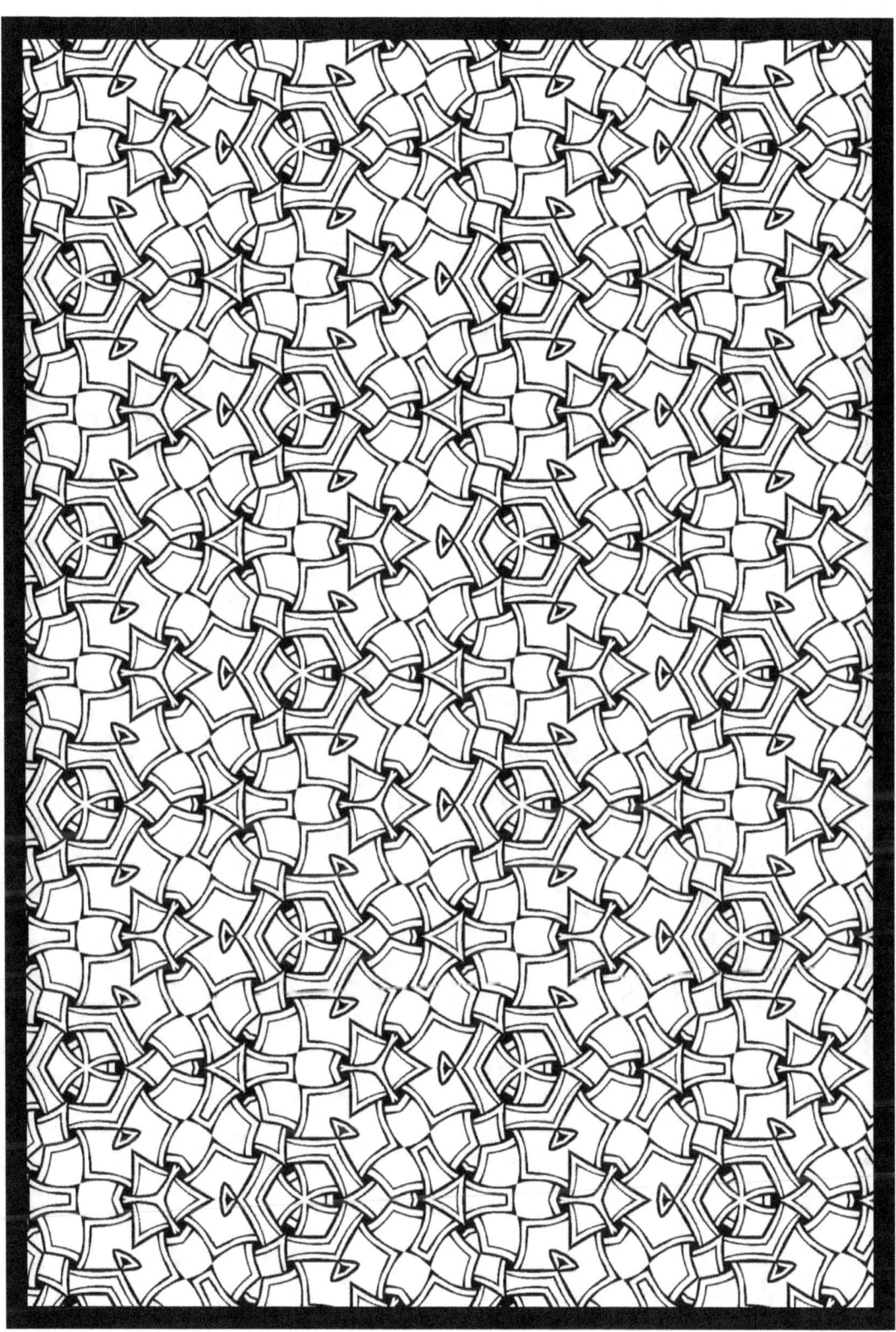

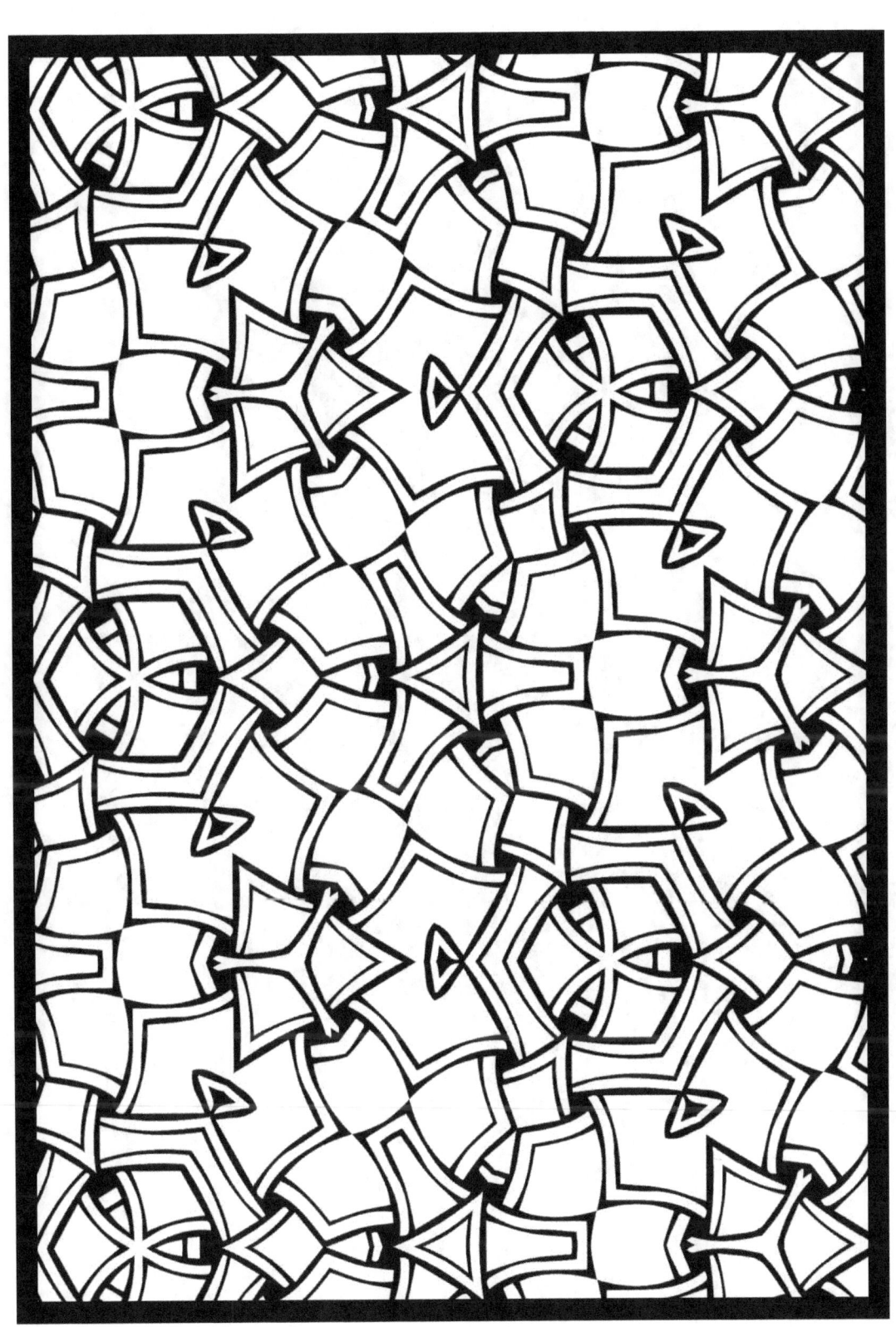

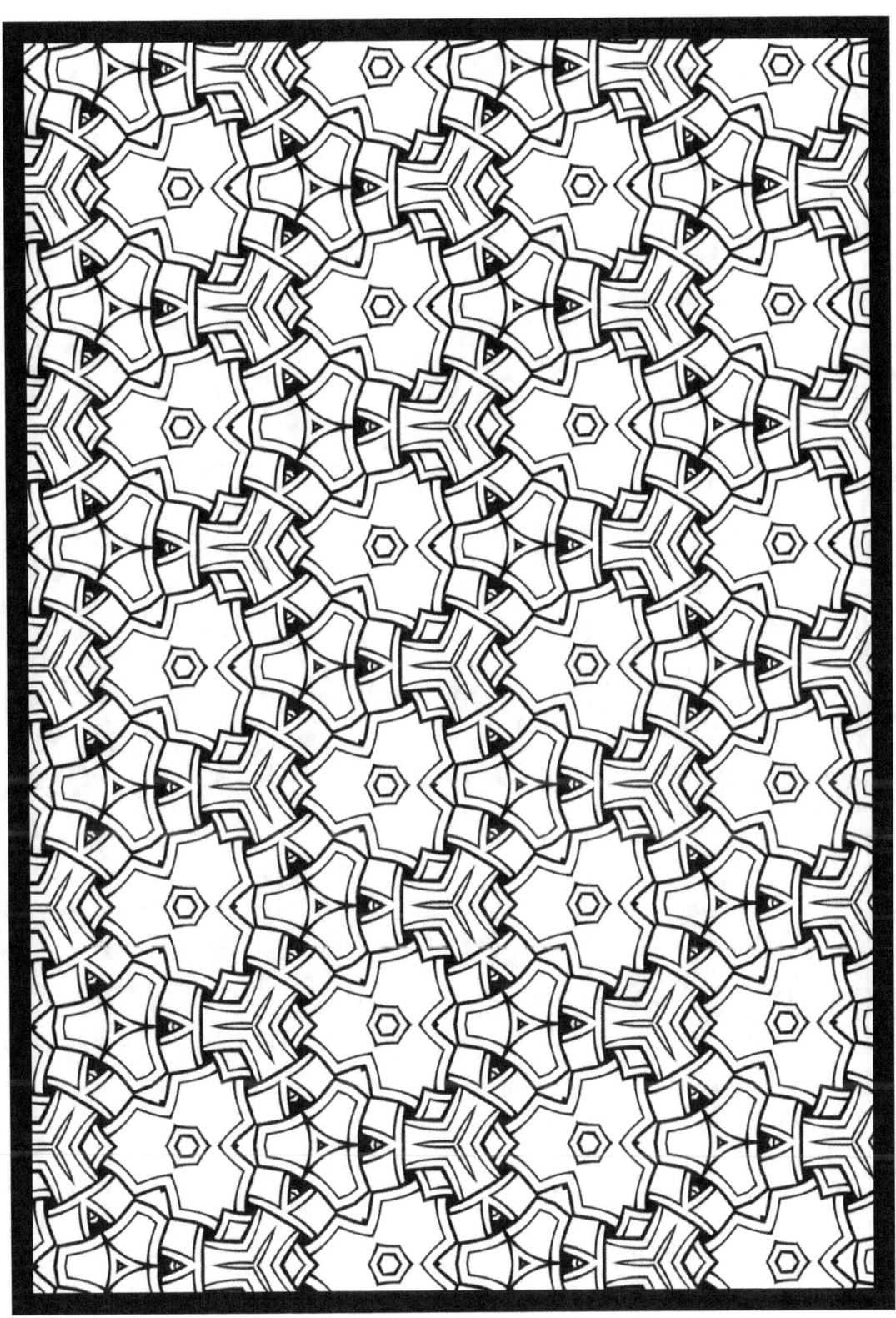

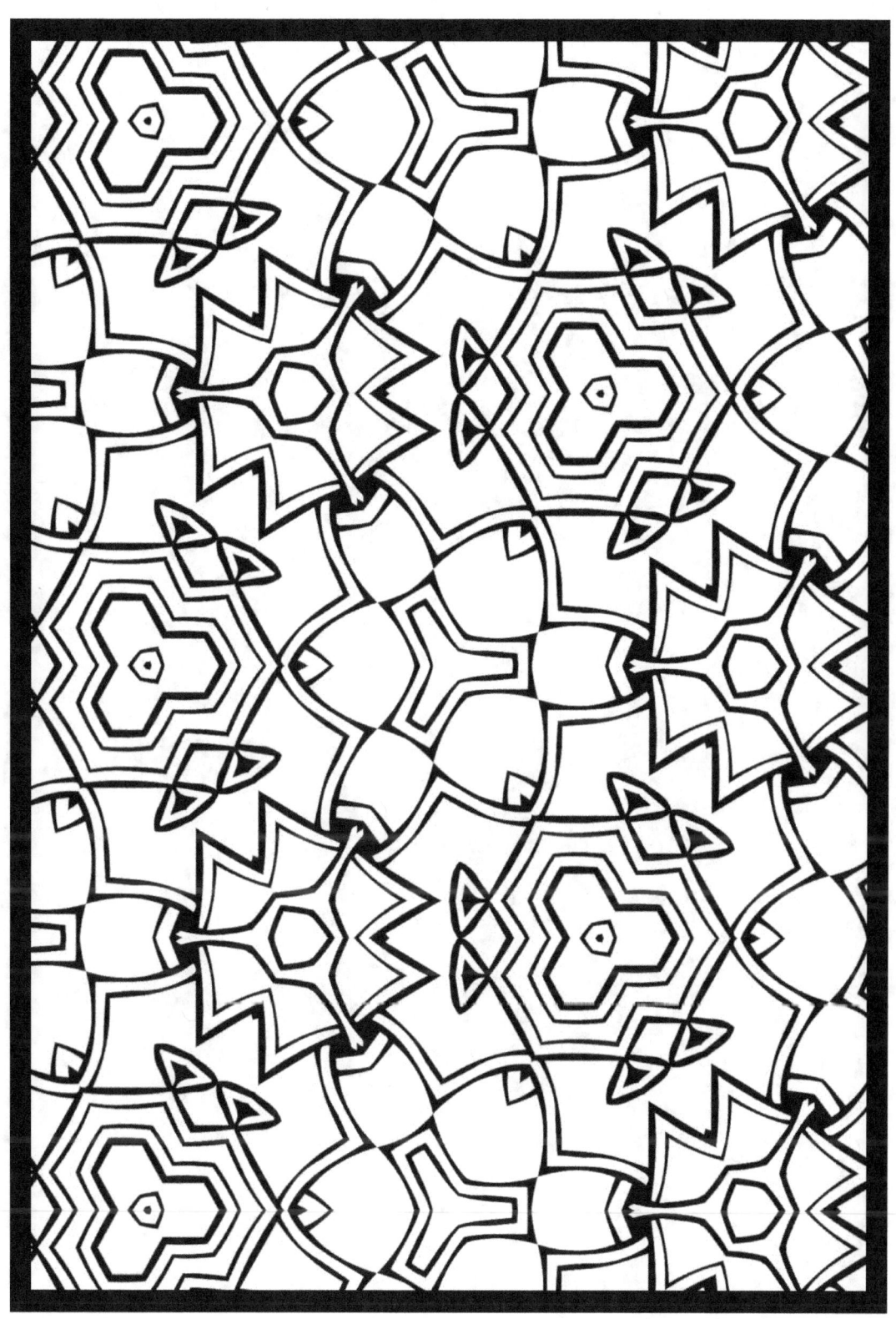

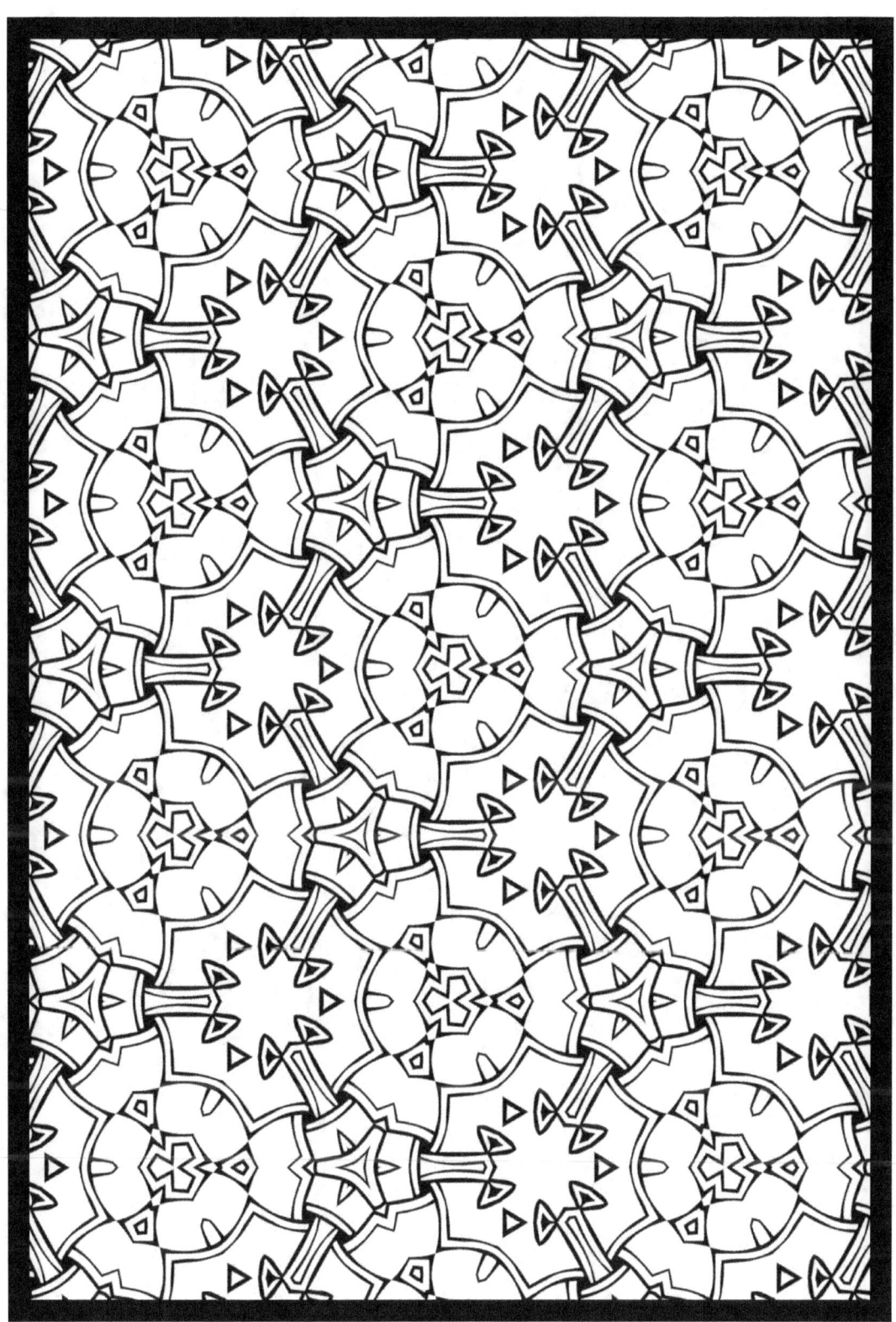

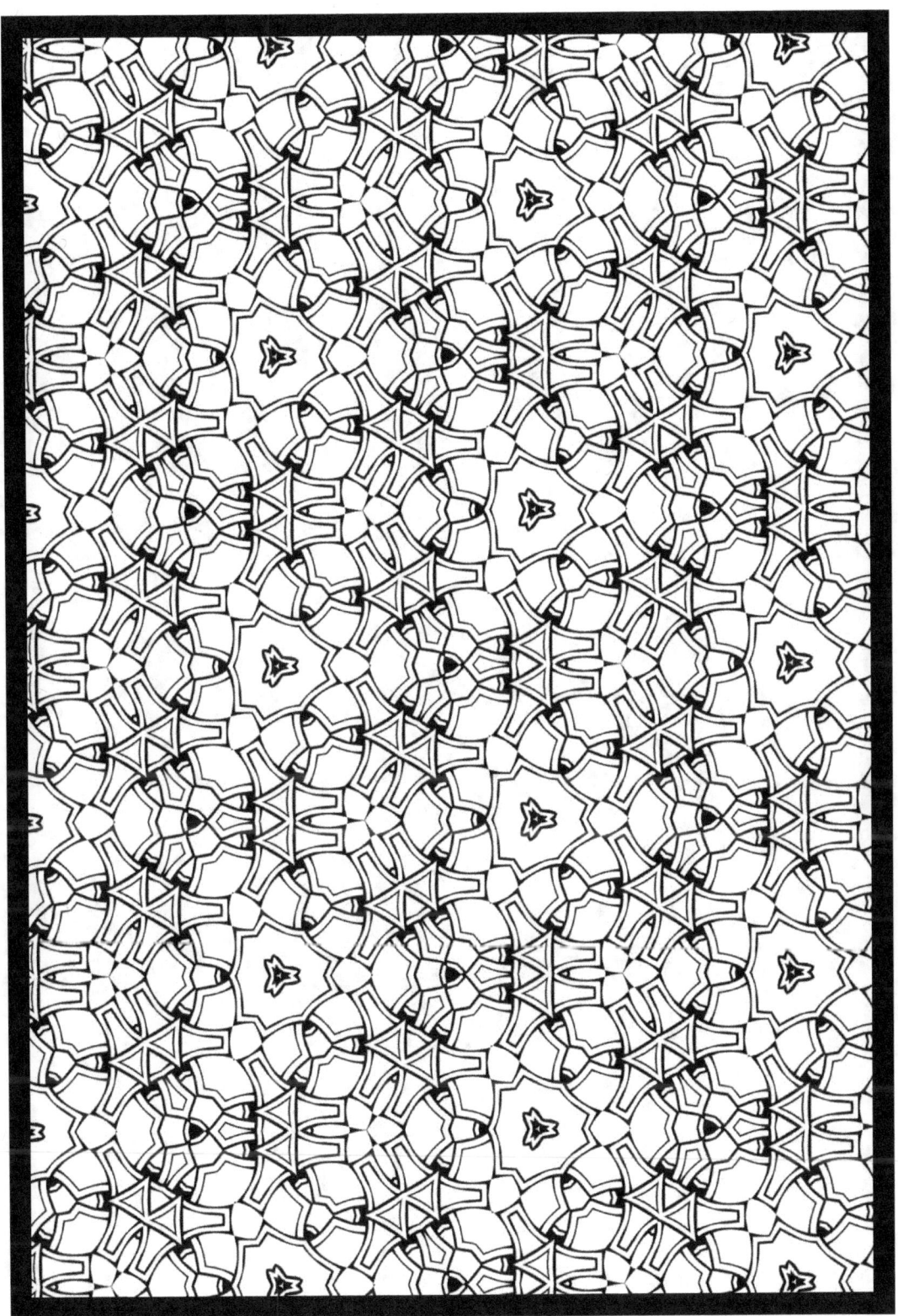

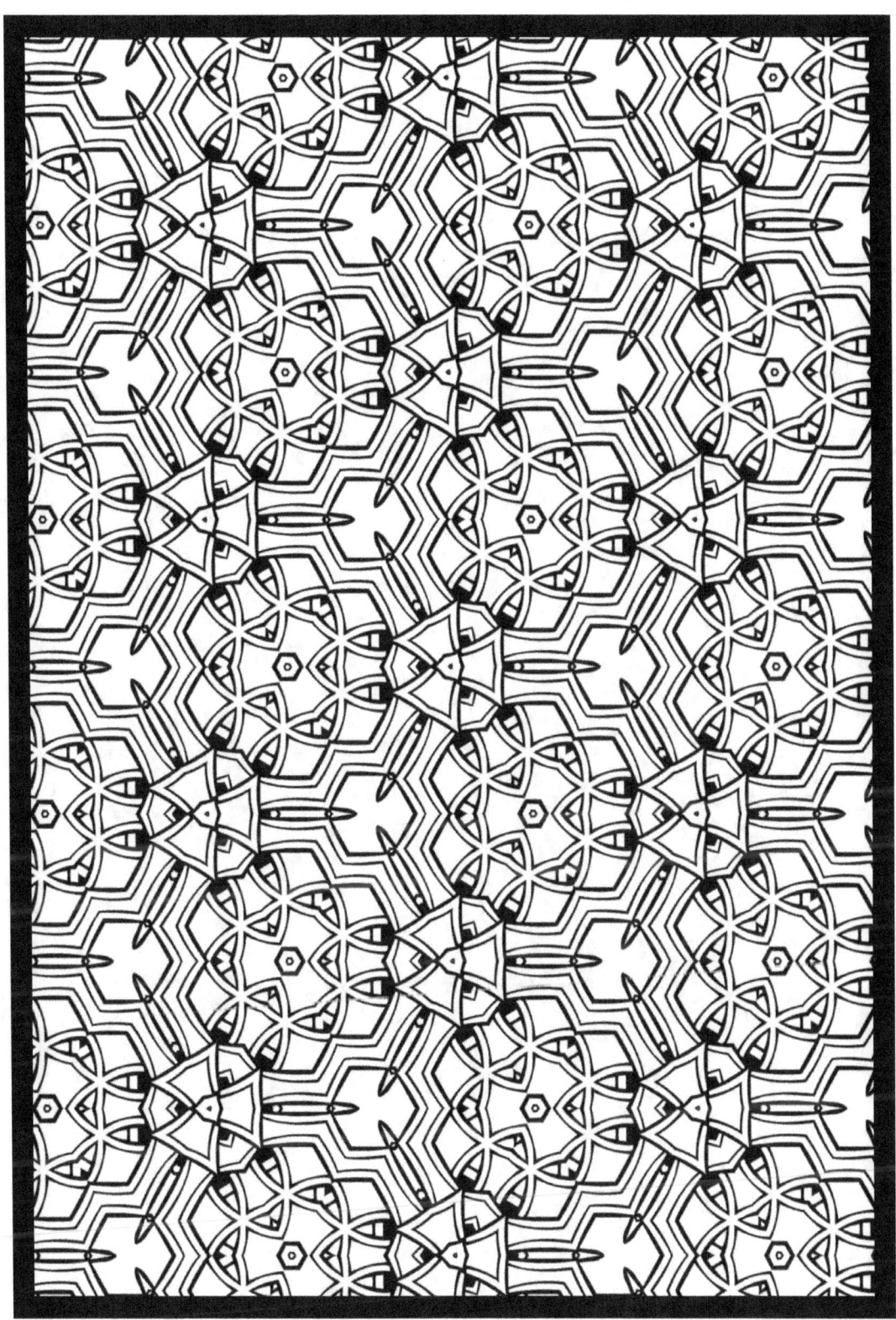

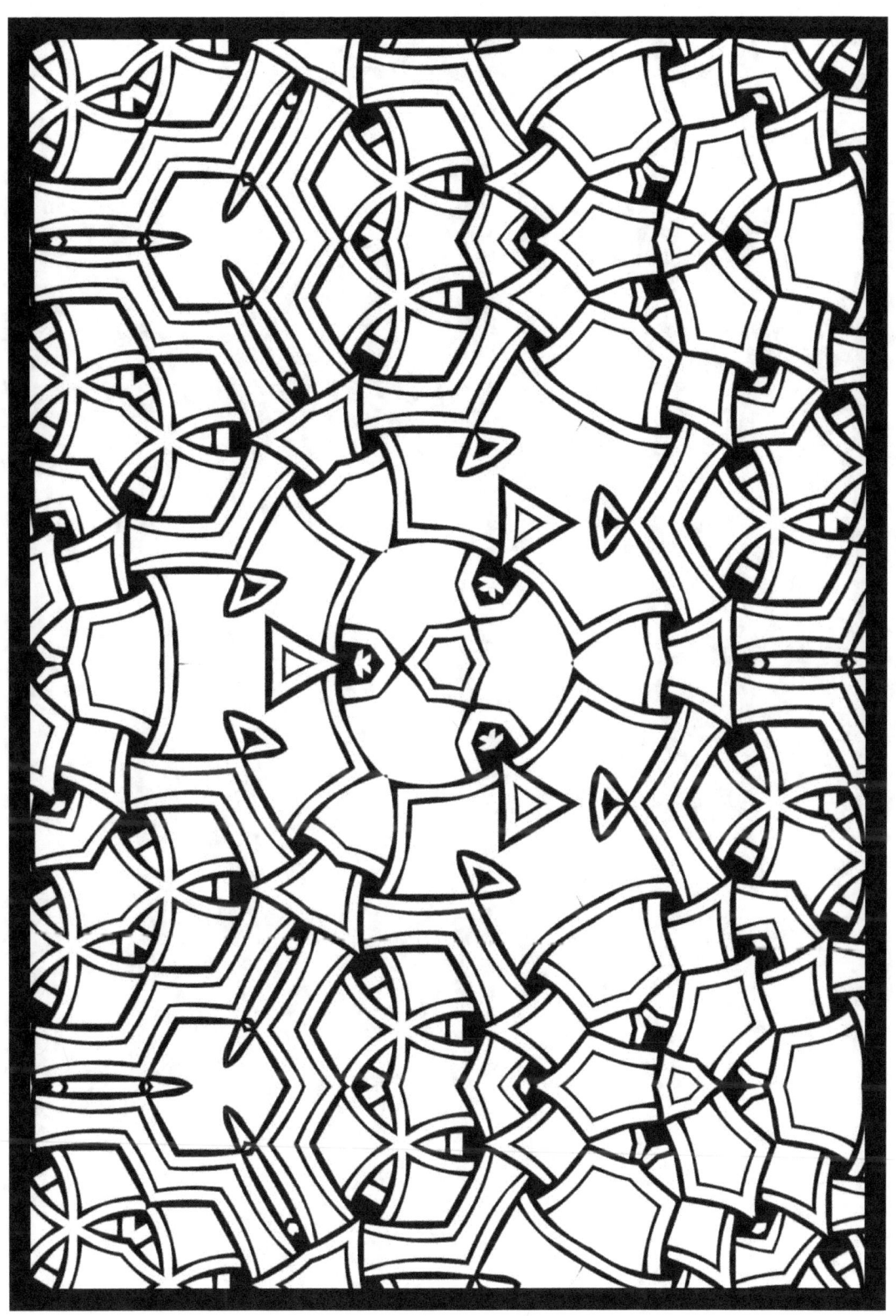

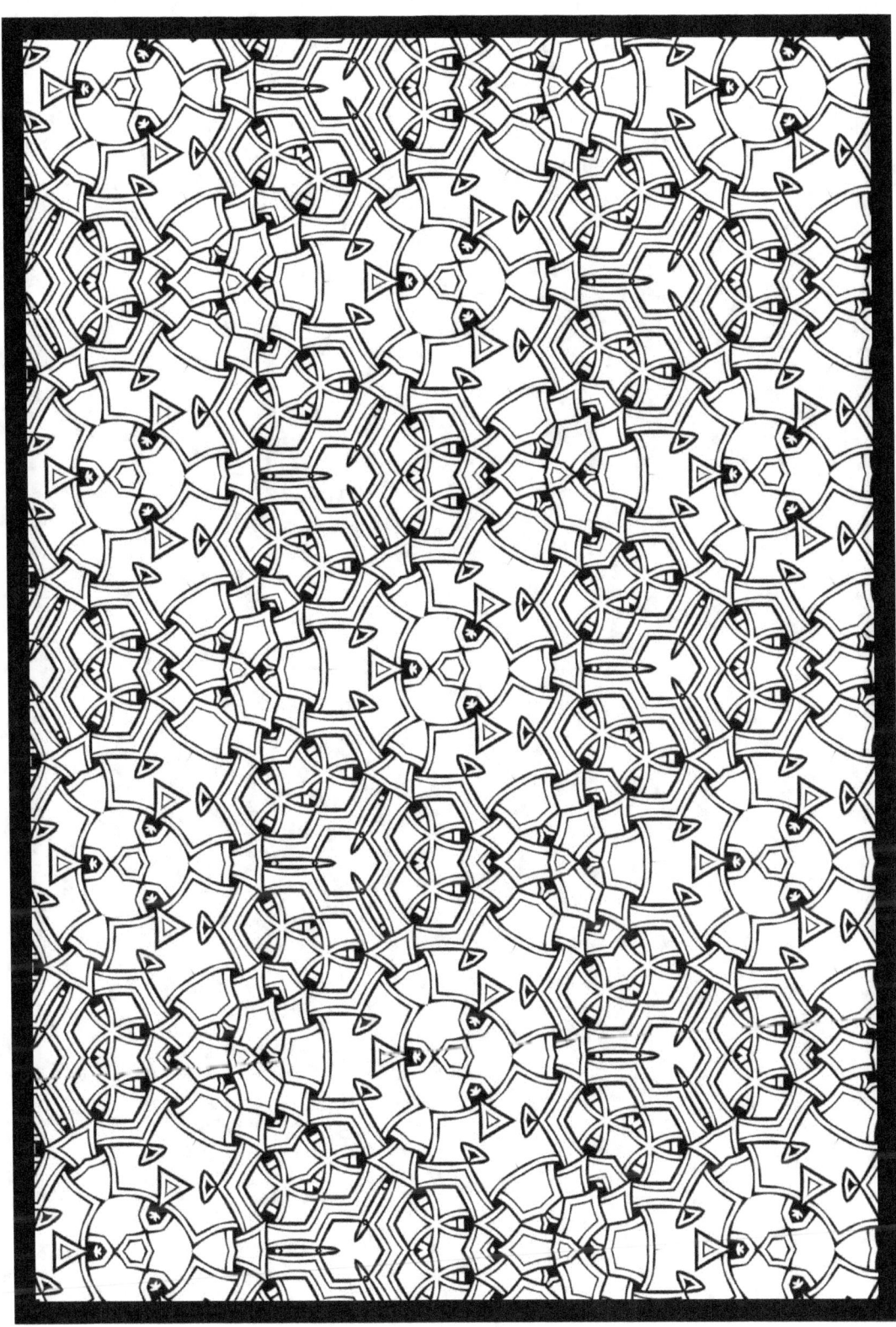

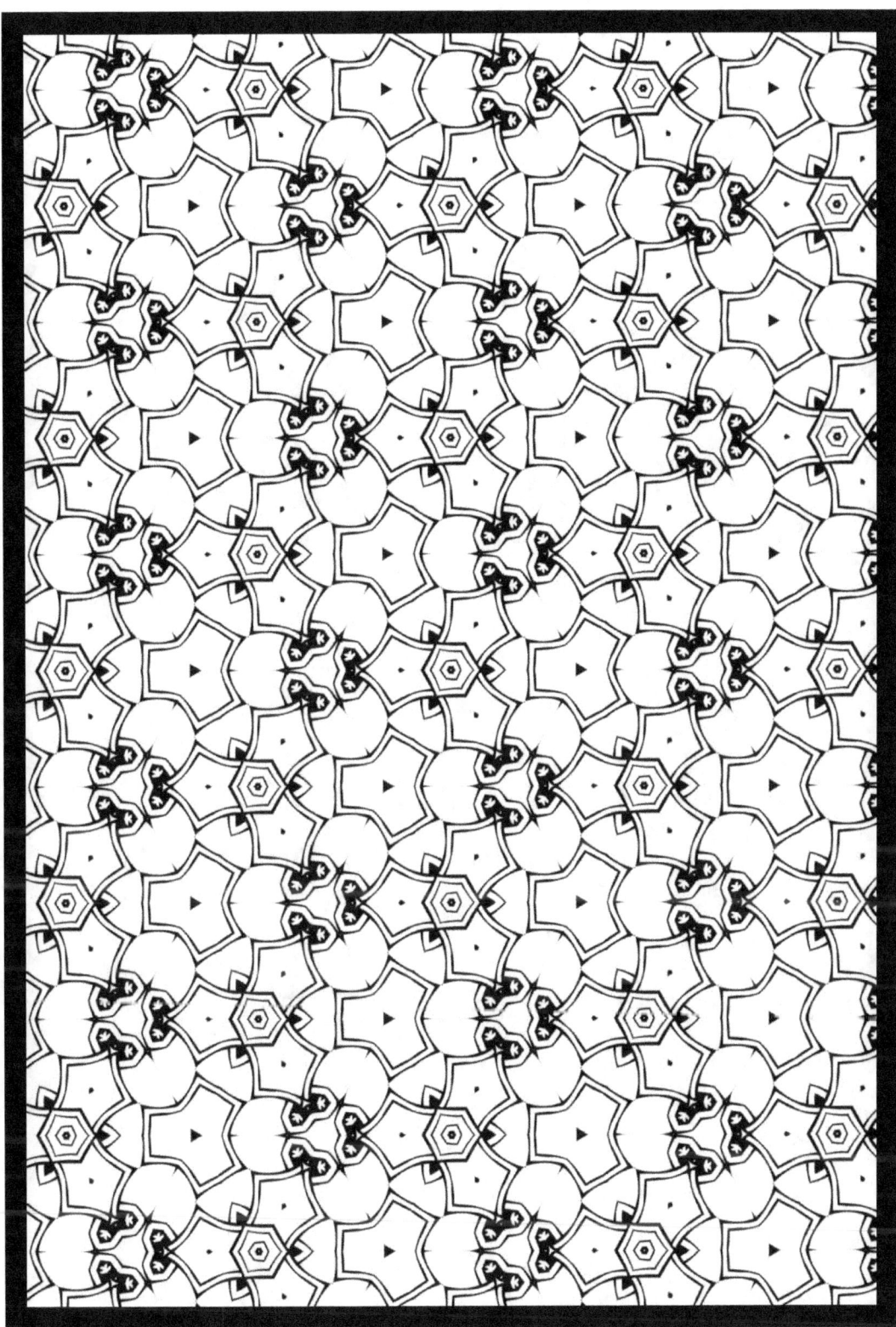

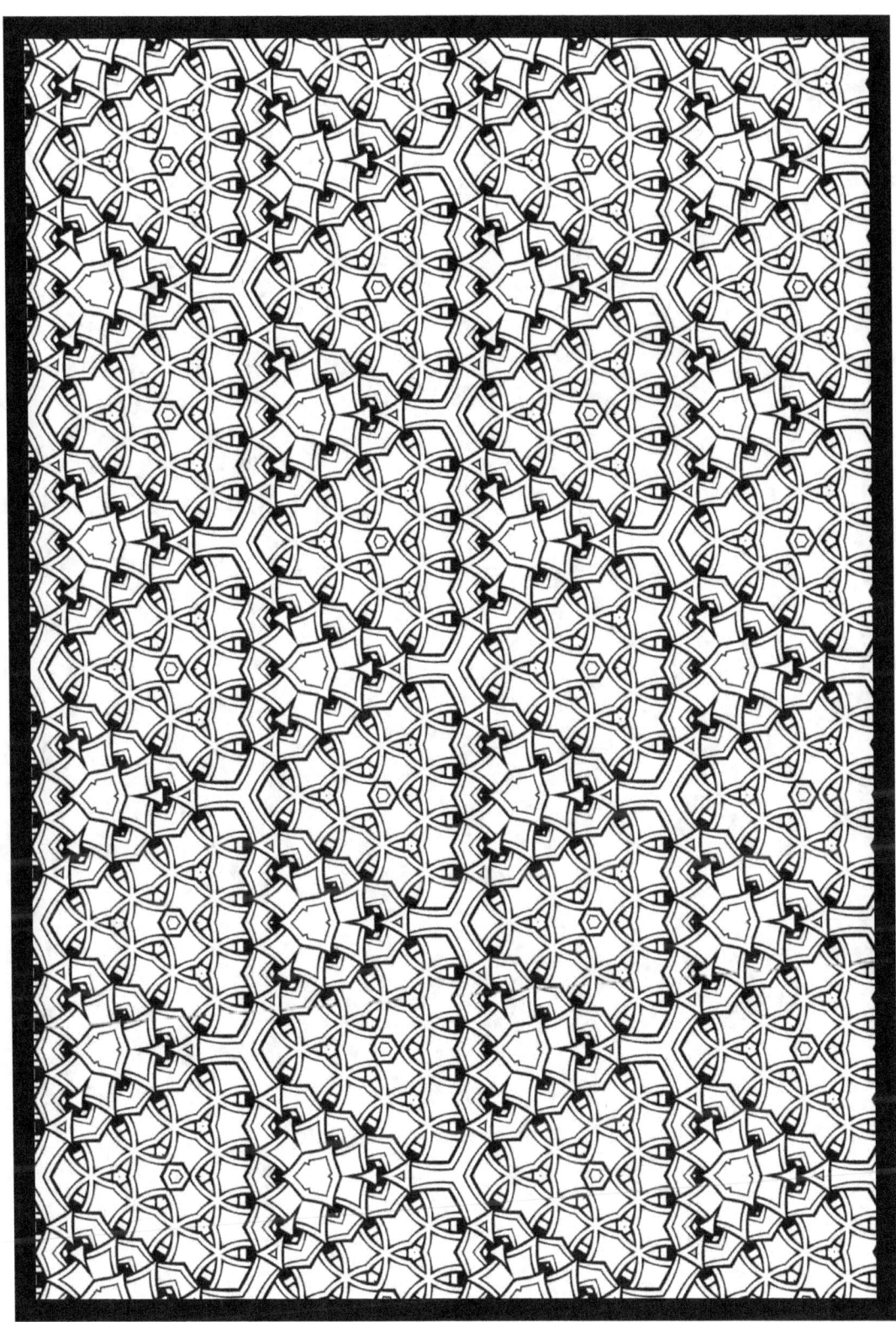

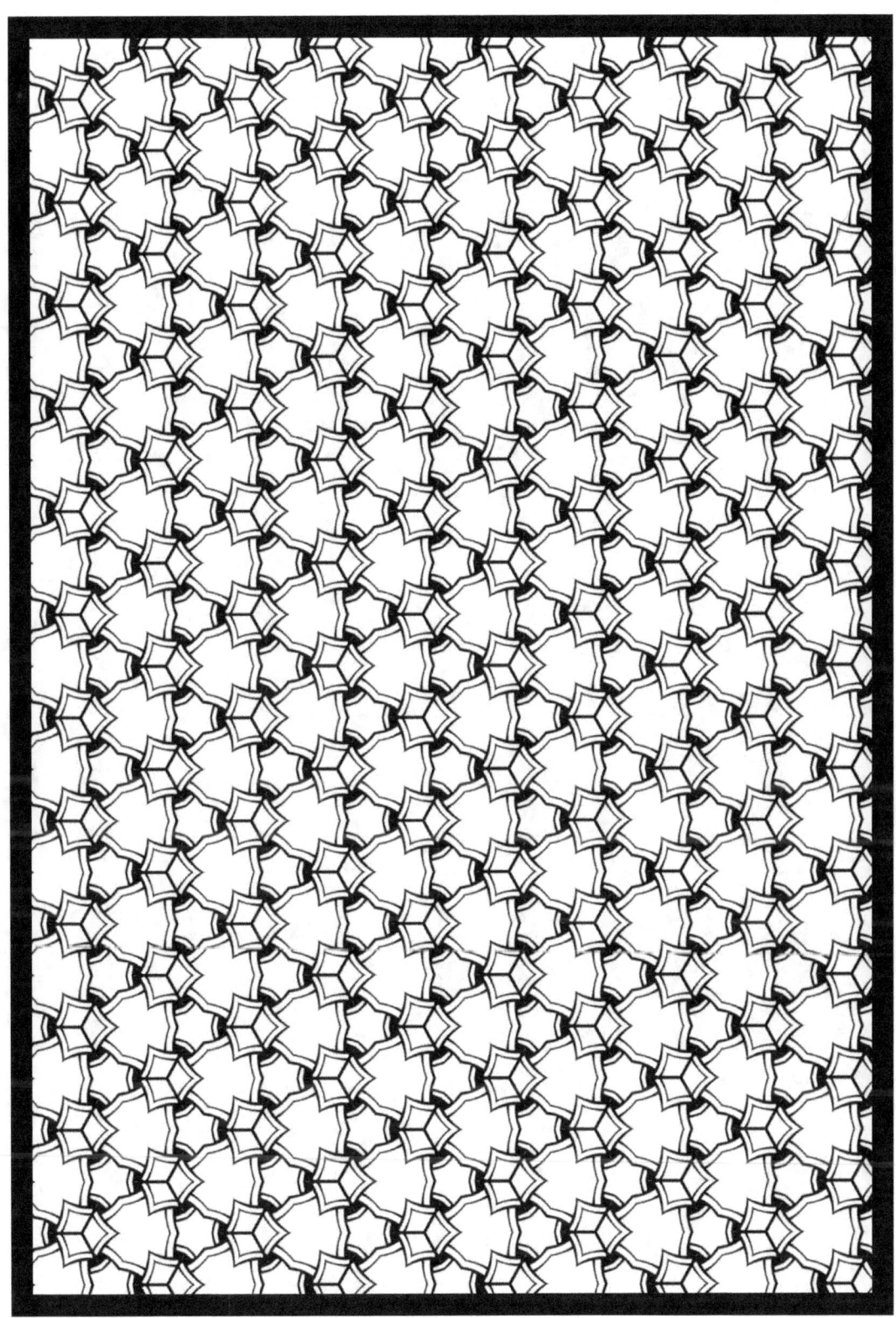

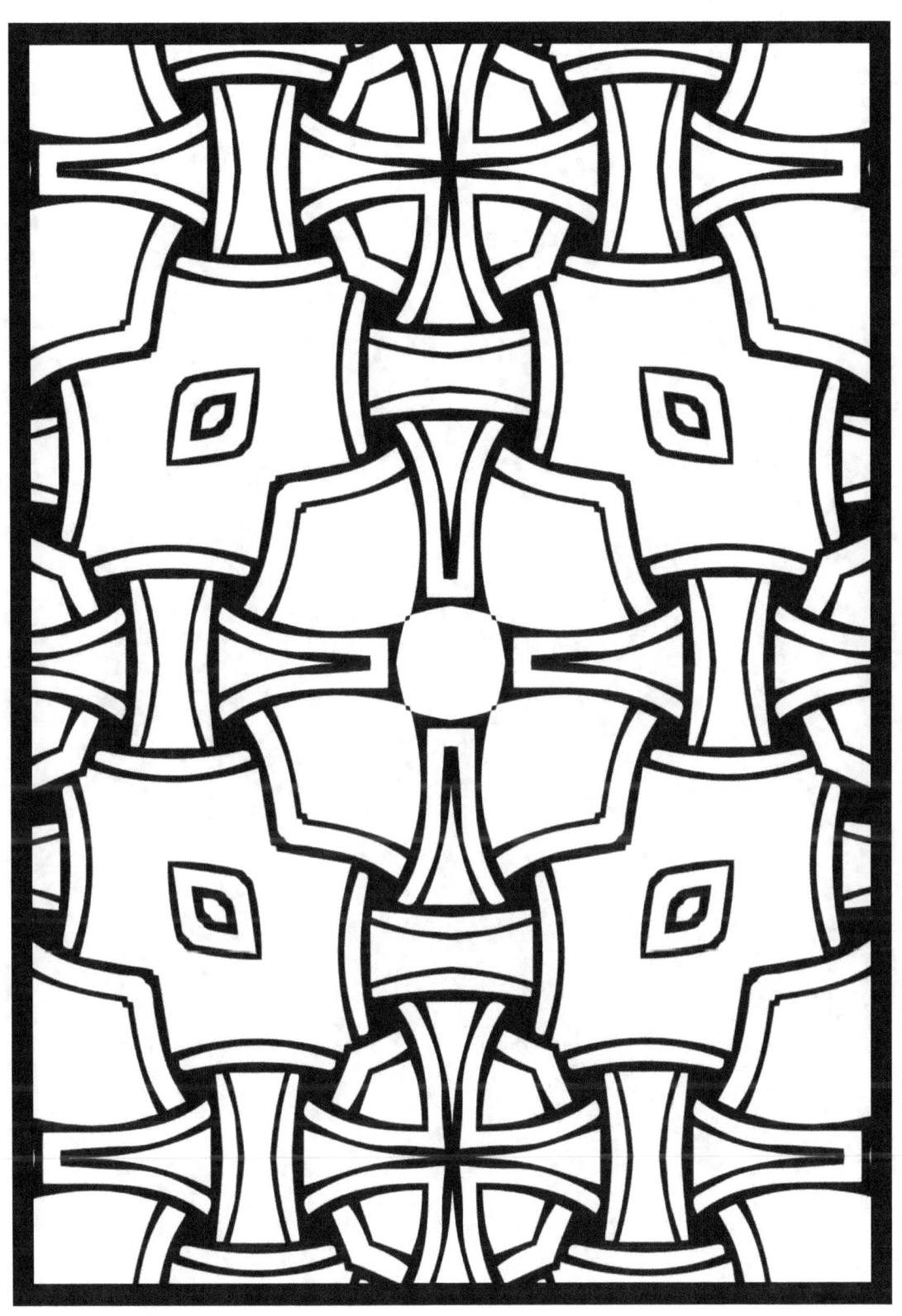

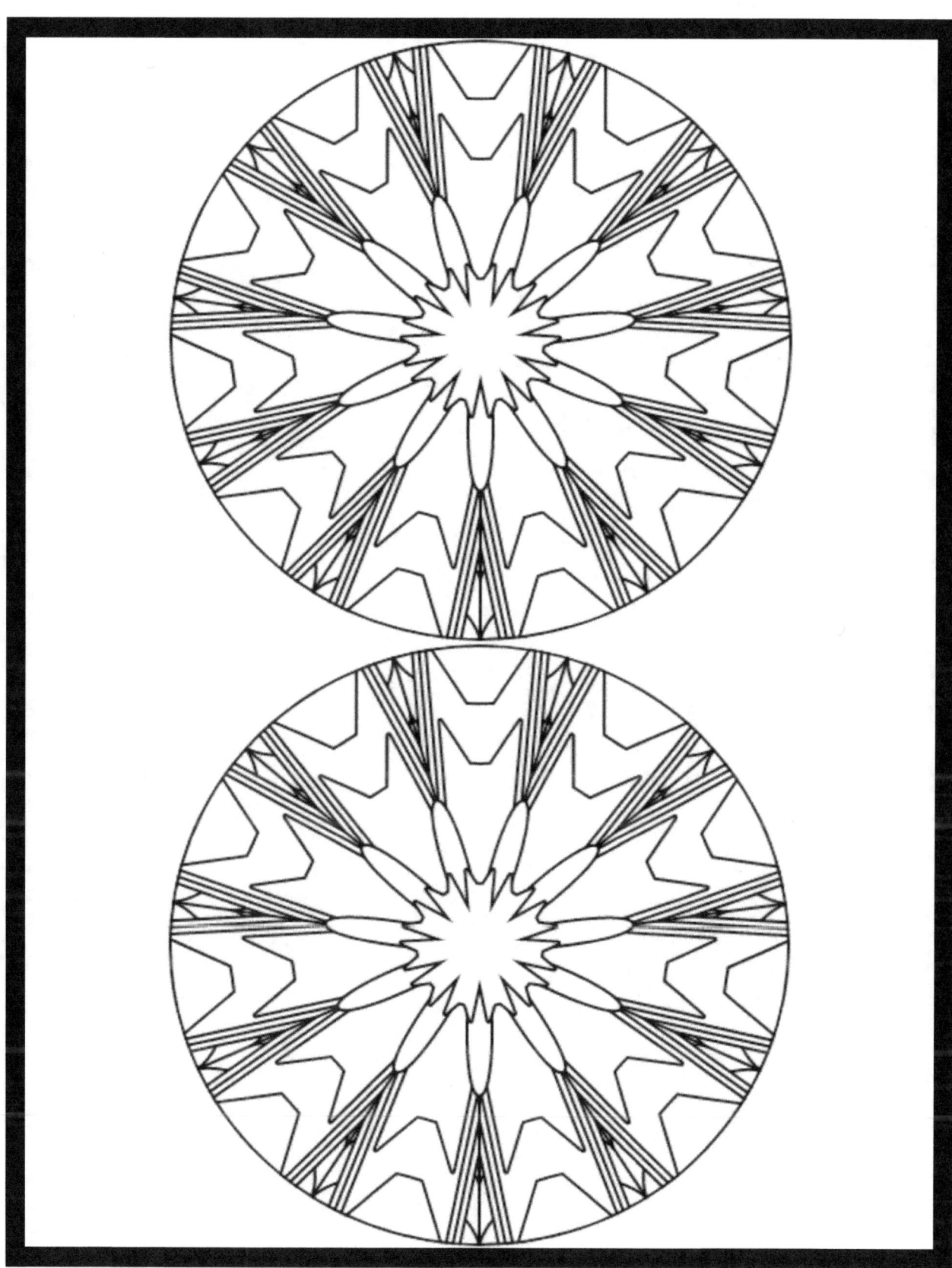

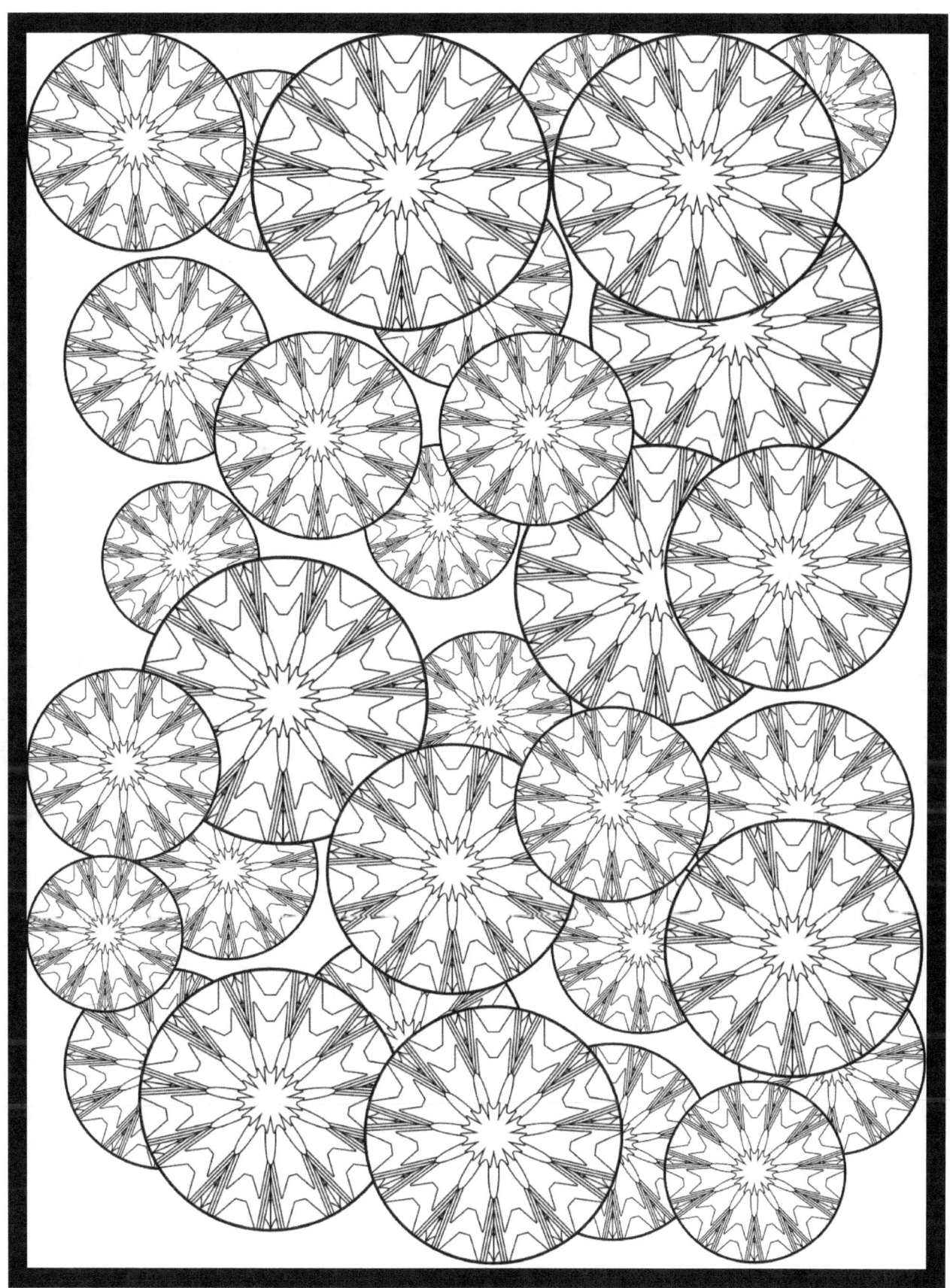

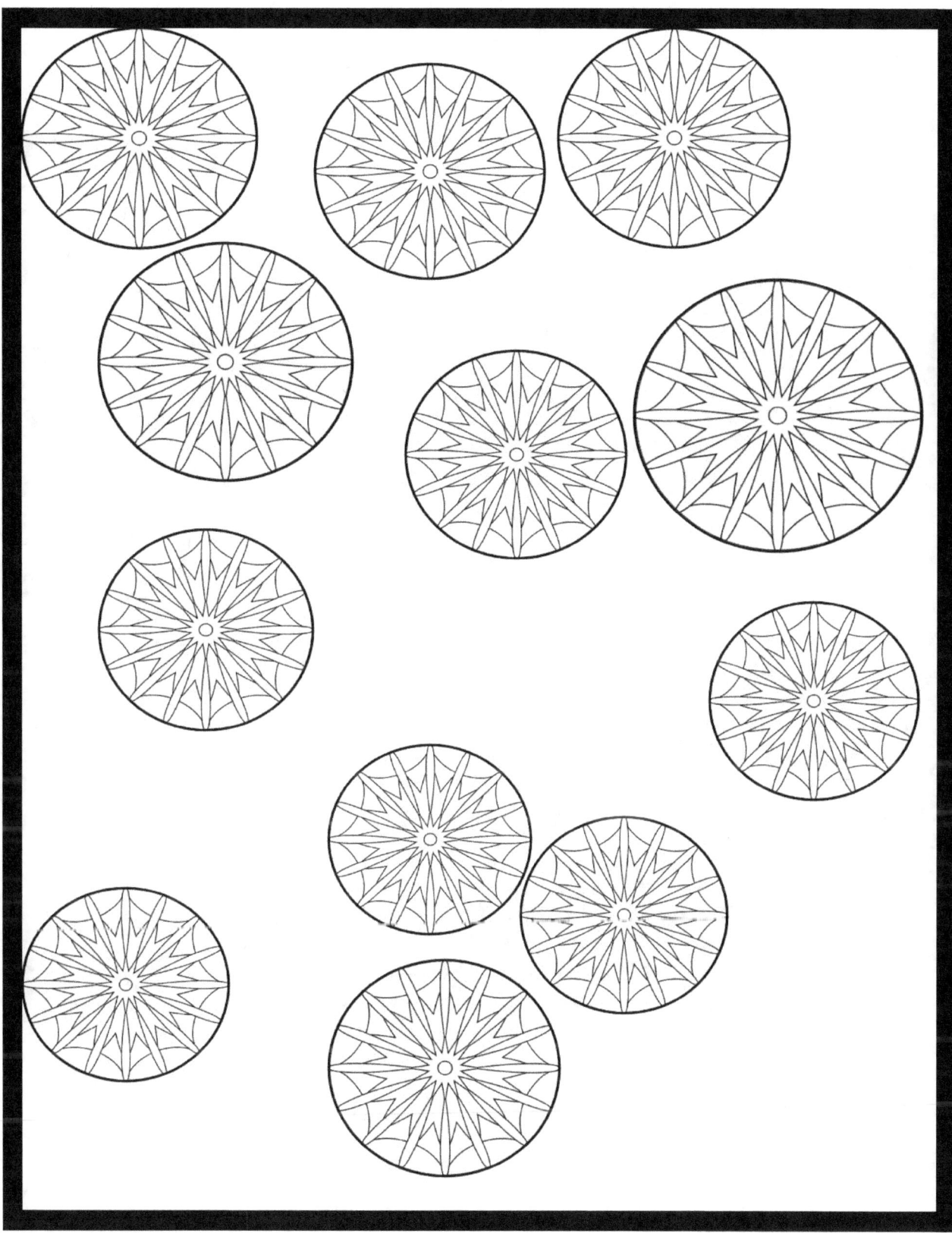

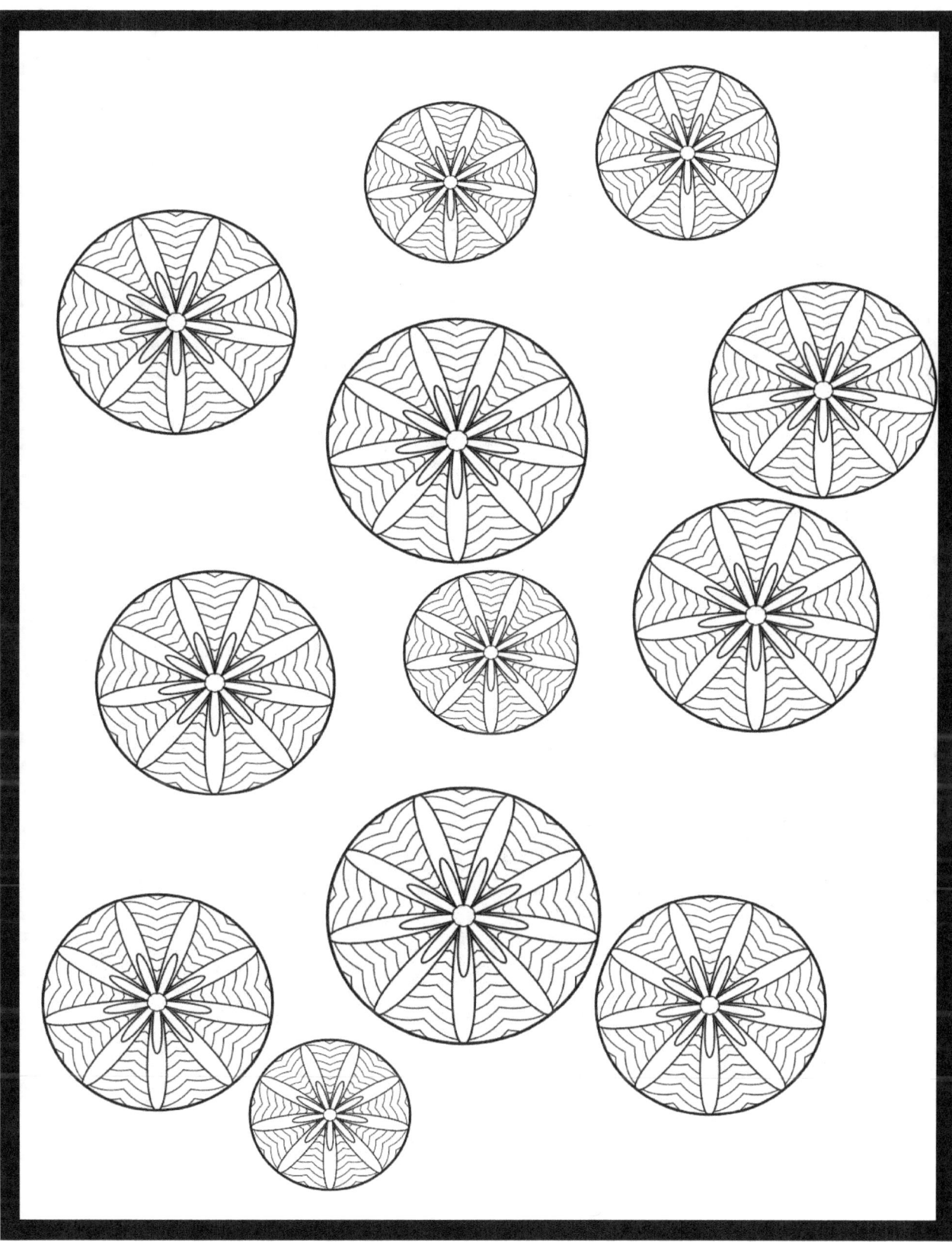

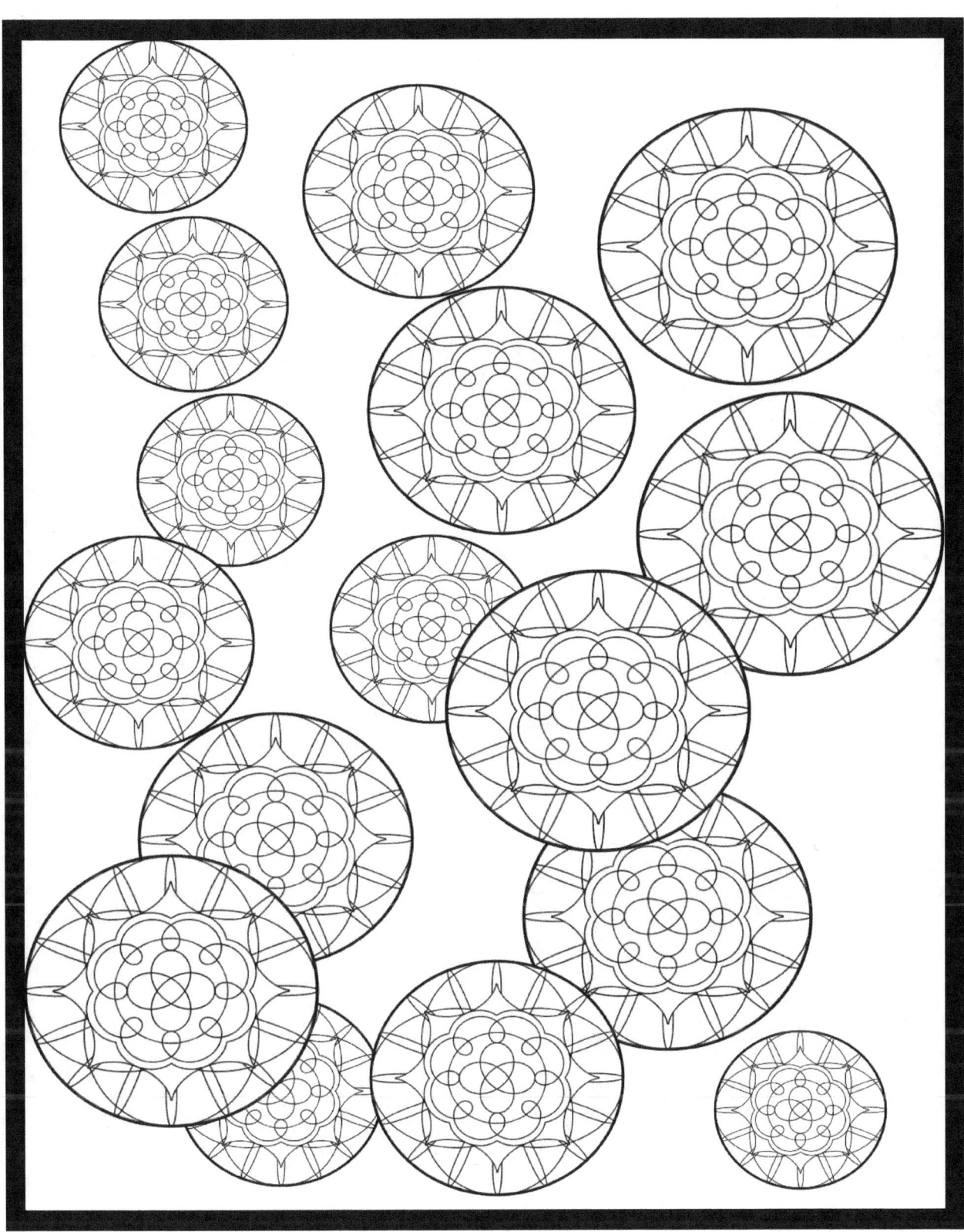

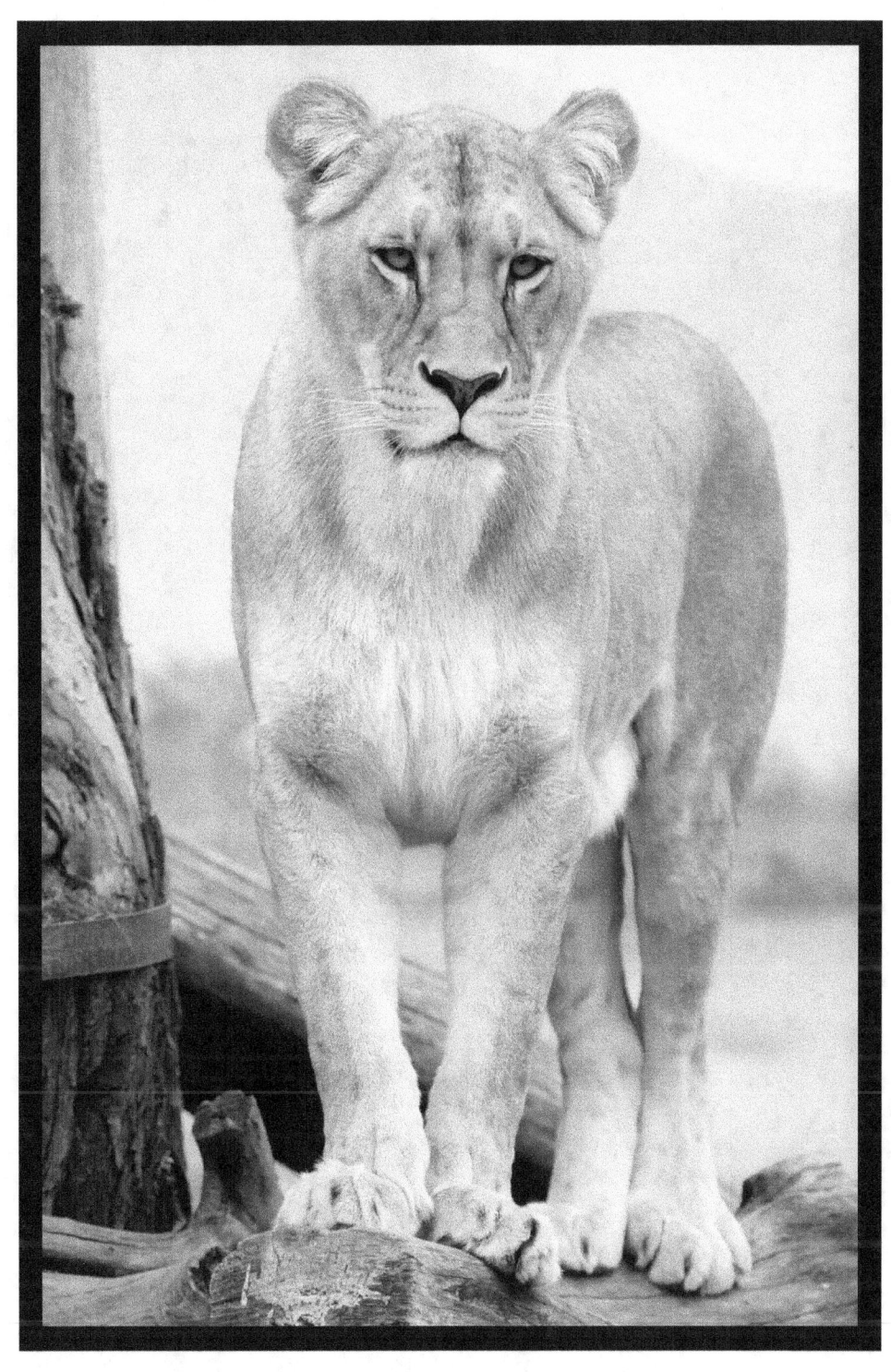

30 Days of Coloring Books for Kids and Adults Lovely Lions Grayscale Photo Book: Lovely Lions Book 1

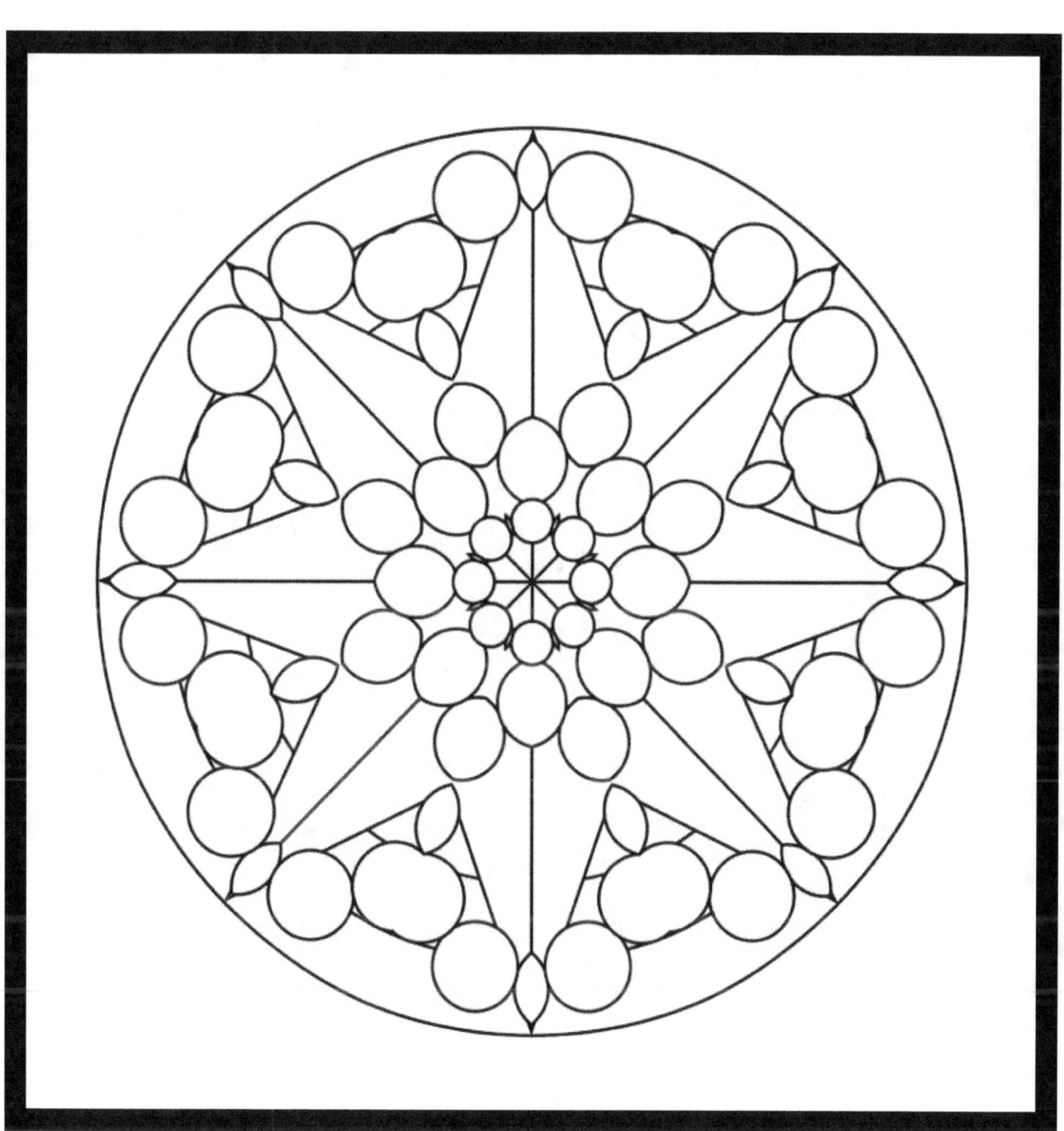

Again thank you for buying this book.

Watch for more as they come out.

Check Gary Wittmann other coloring books.

Great book...

30 Days of Coloring Books for Kids and Adults Lovely Lions Grayscale Photo Book: Lovely Lions Book 1

30 Days Of Coloring Books For Kids And Adults Bearly Beautiful: Bearly Beautiful Grayscale Photo Coloring Book (Volume 3)

30 Days of Coloring Book for Kids and Adult Dubois County Portrait Pictures: Dubois County Coloring Book Vol. 1 Portrait Pictures (Volume 1)

30 Days of Coloring Books For Kids and Adult: Coloring Books For Adult (Volume 1)

30 Days of Coloring Books for Kids and Adults Volume 2 Snowflakes: Snowflakes

This book had a Christmas theme...First half of book is coloring for you. The second half is black and while coloring page.

12 Days of Christmas